Also by
Ellen Waterston

POETRY

Between Desert Seasons

Hotel Domilocos

I Am Madagascar

Vía Láctea

NONFICTION

*Walking the High Desert:
Encounters with rural America
along the Oregon Desert Trail*

Where the Crooked River Rises

WE COULD DIE DOING THIS

DISPATCHES ON AGEING WHERE LAND MEETS SKY

ELLEN WATERSTON

SOURCE MEDIA

Source Media
The Source Weekly
www.bendsource.com
Lay It Out, Inc.
704 NW Georgia Ave.
Bend, Oregon 97703

ISBN: 979-8-218-53185-0
LCCN: 2024922370

COVER PHOTOGRAPH
The comet Neowise by Richard Scott Nelson

Dedication
To everyone of a certain age

Do not regret growing old. It is a privilege denied to many.

UNKNOWN

Contents

Foreword

AS A YOUNG PUBLISHER, I met Ellen Waterston when thoughts of ageing and the ticking of my biological clock were far from mind. Our fledgling newspaper had secured a spot at a local coffee shop for a poetry reading event. It was standard open mic-style with an eclectic mix of poets delivering their sometimes-challenging-to-listen-to works of art. When Ellen took the stage, our humble gathering was transformed by her confident tone while speaking eloquently in meter about the inter-mountain west. It has been almost thirty years since that evening, but I still remember it well for shedding light on the quality of talent that can grace a small community and for the friendship and professional relationship that developed from that moment and continues today.

Ellen has written for our publication, *The Source Weekly*, since the paper's inception in 1997. We have proudly reprinted excerpts from her books, and she has recounted stories for the community within our pages. It was her opera, *Vía Láctea: A Woman of a Certain Age Walks the Camino*, that opened a window on ageing that piqued our editorial team's interest. While the work is fiction, Ellen's perspective gained from walking Spain's Camino de Santiago is not. If you are not familiar with the work, it is a story crafted from her time spent following the footsteps of Middle Age prophets who walked before her on the Camino in Spain.

The opera dovetailed into my life with similar stories my mother had been sharing about the prejudice women experience entering their later years. At the time, the stories were humorous, but they had an edge that let me know there was a measure of anger and disbelief about the indignities she was encountering as she grew older. Once the window was opened it was hard not to see the lack of respect that the generations in front of us experience as well as the myriad number of small slights that can make up a day.

So, when Ellen approached me about publishing a column on ageing in our newspaper, her request fell on sympathetic ears. It might seem incongruous that a newspaper that thrives on its nightlife calendar would be a good medium for a column on ageing but somehow it works. "The Third Act" has been a reader favorite since its first printing in March 2021. If we have learned anything from the pandemic years, it is that prejudice exists in many forms and is primarily derived from an ignorance of another's circumstance. Ellen's column is an honest, humorous look at the hidden stereotyping I believe we all perpetuate unless we stop to look ahead and understand the fleeting privilege of youth.

Aaron Switzer
Source Media
Bend, Oregon

Preface

AFTER MY SIXTY-FIFTH BIRTHDAY, it wasn't so much the signs and symptoms of ageing (though they were/are there) but rather how diminished the negative messaging about being old in America made me feel, particularly as a woman. So, I did what I do when I am confounded by a situation. I ask myself what is the bigger invitation of this moment at this time in my life? How can I respond? How can I shape the questions contained in that invitation into something useful to others or, at the very least, entertaining? A blank sheet of paper and pen generally figure in my effort to articulate the answer to just about everything. In this case, I started by listing topics related to ageing and ageism, with the goal of reminding fellow oldsters how invaluable each of us is to our families, communities, the future of this country, this planet...and therefore must be to ourselves. I felt compelled to share what my research and reading revealed about an extraordinary time of life that wasn't contained in the never-ending ads for every failing body part.

I contacted *The Source Weekly* to see if they'd consider running a column on the topic. In addition to my enormous admiration and respect for founder and publisher of Source Media, Aaron Switzer, and *The Source Weekly* editor, Nicole Vulcan, I also knew I'd need a deadline to hold me accountable. And then there was the appeal of a column on being old in a groovy newsweekly oriented toward a much younger set.

These dispatches first appeared in *The Source Weekly* over a three-year period. Some are specific to Bend or the surrounding high desert but hopefully apply to anywhere America and beyond. Some are specific to certain dates or events but hopefully the message they carry remains current. Above all, taken together, may they provide perspective and a few laughs as, shoulder-to-shoulder, we seniors navigate this new territory called old age.

Ellen Waterston

SPRING

How old would you be if you didn't know
how old you are?

SATCHEL PAIGE

CHAPTER 1

Metaphormosis

DURING THE FIRST HALF OF LIFE, as author James Hollis writes in *Finding Meaning in Midlife*, we are, appropriately, concerned with the external: what does the world ask of me as professional, partner, parent? In the second half, the focus changes, becomes an inside job: what question do I answer with my life?

Actually, regardless of your age, I'm persuaded the sooner you start the second half of life the better, as I think it asks the more important question. However, most avoid it like the plague, associating it with disease, decrepitude, and, dare I say, death.

On the occasion of my sixty-fifth (speaking of time flying...that would be over a decade ago) I got a free lifetime United States Forest Service Park permit. When he handed it to me the young man in his crisp uniform and Smokey the Bear hat smiled and said: "The *pass* will never expire." But here's the thing. That Forest Service guy failed to take into account one important fact. It's not just the lifetime pass that never expires. Neither do I. I'm not talking ashes to ashes. I'm talking riddles, rhizomes, metaphors. As a writer I *live* in the land of metaphor. My motto? Metaphor-mosis. Change your metaphor, change your life.

I have come to see my life, all of our lives, as part of a linked narrative, like the eighty-thousand-year-old Pando colony of poplars rhizome-ing their way to eternity. I'm but one small daisy in a long, infinite daisy chain. At this age I'm amazed by how little I understand of life and it's precisely that *not* knowing that, on a good day, excites me now.

Sure. Most days I thrash around thinking it's *my* story. I am its author, so why isn't it turning out the way I want? But on good days I see that the real deal is to be on the lookout for the archetypal signs and mileposts that tell me where I am in the story I was dispatched here to tell, not one someone else or some institution tells me to live or my ego leads me to believe I'm authoring. This is a stretch, I know.

How did I arrive at this perspective? If I look at my life so far: New England, New York City, world travels, the ranching West, and now, after a few personal and professional non sequiturs, here I am in this high desert town thinking about metaphor-mosis and life never-ending? You can't make this stuff up. I can't either. So who is?

Hollis says each of us is a crucial part of "a great unfolding. Something is living us more than we are living it. We don't create ourselves, we happen to ourselves. We don't make our story, our story makes us." The world, as Muriel Rukeyser said, is not made of atoms but of stories. I say we can't see the pattern that is our life or the pattern of the whole but must, on faith, believe it exists and fulfill our obligation to complete, as elegantly as possible, our small square of the cosmic quilt. As W.H. Auden wrote: "We are lived by powers we pretend to understand." Or Robert Frost: "The afternoon knows what the morning never suspected."

As I have made my way through "my" life, over and over again I have been confronted with challenges that demanded this Ms. Potato leave the couch of false comforts, false perceptions, false metaphors and venture into uncharted territory. And now, as a woman of a certain age, that uncharted territory includes having the courage to look out across the inscrutable vastness of this narrative I'm part of.

Regardless of age, at some point all of us feel despairing, unworthy. One reason might be that when things really do or really don't work out (they're the same thing, by the way, they both bring us to our knees either in gratitude or supplication), we take all the credit or all the blame. Another reason is that we haven't caught on to the fact that a story is living *through* us and that we must make every effort to be in service to that telling. We forget that the source of the wound becomes the source of the divine, however you define divine, and that the grit and grime of hardship is just the beginning. It's the beginning of an alchemical process that creates the base matter that ultimately becomes your personal gold, your unique contribution to the mono-myth: the hero's and heroine's journey. What's in your story today?

CHAPTER 2

Time Travel

THANKS FOR HANGING IN THERE for a second look at this notion of "Change your metaphor, change your life." I posit that once we do it's just possible we're no longer under the spell of the borrowed story, of the temporal and cultural myths that boss us around. See you later memory, beauty, gut, bone and muscle supplements! Adiós "too late," "too old!"

At some subconscious level, don't we know we are part of a bigger question, a bigger answer, a bigger narrative? Doesn't that explain why our dreams are filled with monsters and angels, and why we, in our dreams, find ourselves either stuck to the ground or flying free? These nighttime odysseys tap into a fundamental, ancient and eerily familiar aspect of ourselves...cowardly lions, heartless tin men. Haven't we, in certain situations, needed some fairy dust, a magic lantern? And when it showed up, what form did it take? Could we *ever* have predicted? What in the world makes anyone think this amazing cycle suddenly stops?

Just for the fun of it, let's change out our belief that life occurs between the metaphors of birth and death and instead be on the lookout for configurations of experience and intersections of time that point a different way. Let's not succumb to the cultural message that time is running out. That there is a "real time" to be "in." Time itself is a metaphor. If we lose a day flying to China, where exactly does it go? Lost two years to COVID-19? What became of them? We had to give up our "metaphor" for what those years would look like, had to adapt, pivot, see the invitation in what took place instead, but no concrete thing was "lost."

Time travels. Time stands still. Time runs out. Time's up. Time's too short, too long. Time's awastin'. A beloved rancher friend once shared his homegrown theory about time, which I reported in my collection of essays, *Where the Crooked River Rises*, and repeat here. He said when you're young, very young, "time goes by real slow but the metabolism is hell bent. As you get older, time speeds up and the metabolism slows down considerable. At death's door," he continued, "the metabolism stops altogether, and yet time goes by so fast all your life's experiences flash before you in one single, fleeting moment." I can picture, as if it were yesterday, how he removed his sweat-stained cap, slicked down his gray hair with the hand missing a forefinger thanks to a run-in with the tractor, and, carefully repositioning the cap back on his head, asking me: "What do you make of that?"

Good question. I've been turning it over until the edges are worn smooth. Based on what he said, it would seem at some point the arcing ellipses of time and metabolism must intersect and when they do, should be in exquisite balance and harmony. Do you suppose this intersection is a single moment in our life? If so, it must be one of perfection. Orgasmic. How can we know when that single moment is? Or when we're in it? Or is it a particular quality *within* each moment? If I practice, can I stay at that intersection and experience everything that way? Could I experience my whole life in the moment the fly line dances out over the river before it hits the water? Before a baby takes in its first breath on the way to a life-affirming cry? The time between the coyote's laugh leaving its lips and when I hear it on the other side of the valley? Is it the moment just before we express our love—the expression of it waiting backstage anticipating its entry? Can we only recognize these instants in hindsight? Like salt thrown over the shoulder for good luck? Or can we live in the present and immediate knowledge of them eternally, by practicing, by nurturing an awareness that they are always happening around us, until it is the all and only of life? These are some of the questions I'd have liked to ask my rancher friend before he died.

In each moment, we have all the time we need. We can't count on how many moments that will be, but we can live honestly into each one as if it's our last, out from under bossy cultural metaphors, robustly and courageously claiming our own. Anwar Sadat, the President of Egypt from 1970 until 1981, reputedly said, "I will not die one minute before my time." Despite the risky policies he embraced, I'd always thought he meant he was in complete charge of when he'd die. I liked the idea. A lot. But when he was assassinated in 1981, I realized he'd meant he had no control of when his time would come but, at the same time, would not waste a minute worrying when that would be.

CHAPTER 3

BTW, We're Not Going to Get Out of This Alive

UNLESS YOU'RE IN YOUR LATE SIXTIES it's likely this concept hasn't fully registered, excepting for those (and may God bless them) who've prematurely stared down death. But look at the oblivious rest of us go! How we put "forever young" on a pedestal, live as though there's no limit on tomorrows.

Then here comes act three characterized by a palpable, albeit subtle, sea change. Suddenly we get it at a cellular level: there are indeed fewer tomorrows than yesterdays. Suddenly the list of what we can do athletically, physically or mentally grows shorter or, at the least, risk and benefit is considered more thoughtfully. Do I climb up a ladder and clean the leaves from my gutters again this year? Suddenly we get goofy over what we used to miss in our haste—an osprey diving for a fish, the smile of a baby in a passing stroller, time spent with family and friends. It used to be that money, honey, and accrued vacation time was all that was required to go on a trip, to get the ski boat and camping gear out of the garage. Now the organizing principle, the litmus, the most valuable and ephemeral currency are the days you estimate you have left on the planet at your present level of activity and mental acuity. If I have maybe ten, possibly fifteen more years at my current rate of speed, how do I want to spend them? How do I decide? What do I want to accomplish...not prove...but accomplish, pay forward, give back? Who do I want to spend time with? And what about *que será, será*? What about *Om*?

Achieving this balance is hard work. Rub your head and pat your stomach. Fearlessly embrace the known outcome and/but stay Zen, or, as cowboys are fond of saying, keep a deep seat and a loose rein. This culture has a field day reminding older folks they are on the way out, taking up space. Birthday cards and late-night comedians make money on our organ recitals, our atrophy. "He's so old that when he orders a three-minute egg, they ask for the money up front." "You know you're getting old when you get that one candle on the cake. It's like, see if you can blow this out." "You've reached the wonder years...you wonder where your glasses are, wonder what day it is."

Fewer tomorrows. It's a cold draft. It takes energy to not get maudlin, churlish, what's-the-point-ish, regretful, hanging out in the memories of yesterdays, the attics of the past. It takes focus to keep our sense of humor, stay on purpose. The pervasive cultural messaging brainwashes fogies into thinking they are passé, are in urgent need of the latest drugs for ailments they never knew existed, and, given the gruesome side effects, require the courage of a red-eyed lion to try. Oldies are targeted for a new and improved take on sidelining, on ghettoization, in the form of age-restricted and gated communities. An eighty-year-old friend of mine moved out of an assisted living facility, got a condo of her own. "They promised resort living," she said. "For me it was last resort living."

The third act. That it is culturally devalued is a shame. The missed opportunity that older members of a community can be to their communities is a wasted resource. The third act is an act of import not only to the actors but also younger audiences.

I interrupt this broadcast to thank COVID-19. True that. The young got older in wisdom as a result. The pandemic leveled the ageism playing field some. With younger generations forced to go inside, literally and figuratively, forced to get off the treadmill, to quiet, to "be" more than "do," they tasted the experience of being older, make that wiser. Days folded in on themselves. Simple things mattered more. The youngers now have a fresh appreciation of what was taken for granted before COVID.

Meanwhile, don't underestimate the over-the-hill gang. Remember, this age group is made up of card-carrying members of the 60s and 70s. They write their own ticket, are still hard charging on behalf of their communities, still claiming their place as entrepreneurs, artists, and thought leaders, still engaged in environmental, cultural, political, and social service initiatives. From cuddling preemies at local hospitals, to planting trees in burn areas, to feeding the homeless. Geezer jocks hit the slopes, coach high school teams. Members of Bend's Vocal Seniority make good trouble. These oldsters are taking country singer Toby Keith's refrain seriously: "Don't let the old man [or woman] in." The patina of their lives reflects their hard-won understanding that, while it's not over until it's over, it's over before you know it. They bring what matters to the table, so set yourself a place. Everyone will benefit.

CHAPTER 4

A Long Way from Lupercalia

IF YOU THINK THE HISTORY of Valentine's Day is all about cupids, roses and chocolates, think again. Though the origins are obscure, what is known is they had more to do with bacchanals and blood.

Blame it on the ancient Romans who, for centuries, annually celebrated the fertility festival of Lupercalia on February 14. Randy male revelers ran naked down the street wielding strips of rawhide from the hides of the dog and goat sacrificed for the feast day. Young women lined up to be whipped, believing it would make them more fertile. The fete concluded with a matchmaking raffle. Maidens placed their names in a big urn and the self-proclaimed bachelors drew one to pair with for the duration of the festival or longer if the match proved a good one.

The ancient Romans are also credited with beheading two saints both named Valentine, both on February 14, both during the third century AD, but on two different years for two different reasons—one for protesting the emperor's prohibition of young men getting married, figuring they made better soldiers if single, and the other for helping Christians escape from the nasty Roman prisons. By the time the fifth century rolled around, Lupercalia had been outlawed as un-Christian by Pope Gelasius. In a gesture toward a more subdued substitute, he lionized the martyrdom of the two saints Valentine with the declaration of St. Valentine's Day on February 14.

By the Middle Ages, the celebration of love begins to look more like the current Valentine's Day. Poet Geoffrey Chaucer penned a Valentine poem in 1375.

> *For this was sent on Seynt Valentyne's day*
> *whan every foul cometh ther*
> *to choose his mate.*

William Shakespeare followed suit.

> *Tomorrow is Saint Valentine's day,*
> *All in the morning betime,*
> *And I a maid at your window,*
> *To be your Valentine.*

During the Victorian era, direct expressions of one's feelings were discouraged so the new.ready-made card helped, though some pent-up feelings were better left unsaid:

> *To my Valentine*
> *'Tis a lemon that I hand you*
> *And bid you now*
> *"skidoo,"*
> *Because I love another –*
> *There is no chance for you!*

Today, jewelry, lingerie, flowers, gift cards and greeting card purchases total roughly twenty-one billion dollars in the U.S. alone! As Valentine's Day is observed by most countries around the world, what's spent globally on wishin', hopin', thinkin' and prayin' has to be astounding.

But you don't have to spend a fortune to celebrate your love. One affordable, delicious and intimate option is to cook a meal together... and not just any meal. The last one hundred pages of Isabel Allende's *Aphrodite, A Memoir of the Senses* are dedicated to dishes claimed to have an aphrodisiac effect. The recipes are ones that Allende's mother cooked for decades but have been spiced up by her daughter based on Allende's research of the history of food as love potion, from hors d'oeuvres ("... tickles and nibbles") to desserts ("the happy ending"). The fun-loving author dedicates "these erotic meanderings to playful lovers and, why not? also to frightened men and melancholy women."

Hold on! For many, one is not the loneliest number. To reinforce that message, February 15 has been designated as National Singles Awareness Day, a day to raise a glass to yourself in celebration and confirmation of being more than enough. But if you are determined to find a mate, best get with the social media program. There's a slew of online dating sites for sixty-five and older, a slew of reviews. Talk to friends and find out what their experience is, which site they favor. All, regardless of age, seem to agree on one thing—it takes determination, conviction, staying power, intention, a nose for nonsense, and a sense of humor. Anecdotal regional polling turns up a few entertaining takeaways. Women joke that men west of the Continental Divide favor images of themselves holding a large, freshly caught fish. There's humorous speculation about what the subconscious message might be. Size matters? I'm a cold fish? I'm into catching and releasing or clubbing over the head and devouring? Both men and women seem to favor posing with their pooch. Apparently, there's bad advice circulating about how to take a good selfie. What is it about bathrooms? So many photos of lonely hearts with a toilet in the background or a sink strewn with all sorts of undesirable information. Having said, those who don't post a photo apparently don't fare well. Those who don't fill in all the blanks of information also trend poorly. Honestly, if you're going to pay for the stress and trouble, might as well go for it!

Yes, the online dating process is more roulette than kismet. But happily single or desperately seeking Susan, we can say we've come a long way from Lupercalia...or have we?

CHAPTER 5

Ribbit

GO AHEAD, CALL ME A BATRACHOPILE, a ranidaphile. You can have your crocus, your yellow blaze of forsythia and daffodil, or the exuberant conk-la-ree song of the red winged blackbird as it heralds its return north. For me the real sign of spring is the sound of the peeper, the tiny, paper clip-sized tree frog that nests all winter under leaves and underbrush next to ponds, wetlands or manmade water features. Not only are these mighty-mites able to live on land or in water, but during the winter their tiny livers flush their bloodstream with what is essentially antifreeze, a cyroprotectant glucose, allowing them to slow their hearts to a state of dormancy until temps get back to a balmy forty degrees. It's then the hooray begins. They hop out of hiding, a balloon of sound fills up their froggy chests and the nighttime hullabaloo gets underway. Though its formal name is Pseudacris Crucifer, another name for this cheery harbinger of spring is, no surprise, Chorus frog.

April is National Frog Month, a tribute to frogs' reemergence in spring. Okay, a bit niche, but the peepers' din does serve to put us on notice that we have another spring to celebrate, new beginnings, new adventures. In the world of spirit animals, frogs represent transition—the successful progression from one stage of life to the next, the capacity to move on from any situation. They come by this reputation honestly, given that their ancestors date back 250 million years.

Most phases or transition periods humans experience as sequential, taking place in the progressive tense...newborn-ing, toddler-ing, adolescent-ing, adult-ing. These are all future-forward names that imply certain expectations and structures. Young adult? Find work and relationship. Mid-life? Skip the crisis and, instead, focus on growing a family, a business, a community. Go! Go!

Then there's retirement. It's what happens after mid-life, post-middle-age, before decrepitude. It's when we're supposed to...pursue leisure until the end of life? It's a bit amorphous as a phase, lacking in definitive cultural or social expectations. And the never-ending-fun model doesn't work for the vast majority of sixty-five-year-olds who either prefer a different approach or can't afford to take off the work mantle, or both. In both cases they're the richer for it, if you're to believe reports on the benefits of staying engaged and on purpose. The words "retire," "retiree" and "retirement" derive from the French *retirer*, meaning to withdraw, go away. In Europe the common designation is pensioner, conjuring a social dependent who has ceased working, all take and no give. Words shape our reality. Retirement suggests backward motion. Believe it and you will see it. As long as we keep using the word retirement, or even clever wordplays such as "the new retirement," or "refiring," or, a bit more positive, "starting older," a trace of withdrawal, of endings, is still in the air. Given our longer life expectancy, we need a new word for the twenty-plus years of activity after sixty-five, for mapping this uncharted transition territory. Go Magellans!

A word that often comes up when asked to describe the experience of the ageing process is diminishment. The time left is shrinking. We want to take full advantage of it, but all systems are not as go as they used to be, something we now must actively factor in when planning a day, a hike, a vacation or climbing the stairs. If only we could stop the clock. Some think they can. Modern-day Magellans of a different ilk are taking a page from the hibernating peepers, placing their dead human bodies in cryopreservation (liquid nitrogen) or in Biostasis, as it's called. Futuristic scientists speculate they can reverse death by preserving the brain and 3-D printing a new body once that technology gets up to speed. "Once that technology is up to speed" is the operative. Meanwhile, hundreds of bodies lie in frigid waiting around the world.

But without such draconian measures, and, instead, celebrated for the good, bad and ugly of what it is, this phase of life is as rich, complex and dynamic as any before it. It's definitely not easy or peasy. It requires we cope and adapt in ways we never imagined, but when has that not been true? Rather than retiring into the background, maybe the structure and expectation of this phase is to take the center of this age's stage with all the vitality, creativity and contentment we can muster. The Spanish got it right. Their word for retirement is *jubilación*. If you say jubilation fast ten times it almost starts to sound like ribbit! Well, kinda, but you take my meaning.

CHAPTER 6

Old Does Not Mean Addled

WAITING IN THE LOBBY, YOUR NAME IS CALLED. A nurse shows you to the examination room. Annual checkup. "How's it going, young man? How are you doing today, young lady?" What is it about those greetings that rub the wrong way? Patronizing? Saccharine? A thinly veiled sympathy card in acknowledgment of this disease called ageing? The reduction of the older individual to a generic? Imagine ever having greeted Dolores Huerta, Harry Belafonte, Willie Nelson, Jane Fonda, the President or Speaker of the House in this manner. Did their celebrity status command more respect? Yes. But they also never saw their age as a limitation. What about the rest of us?

Nowadays, when I meet total strangers hiking to Green Lakes or Broken Top, they'll say "Good job!" "Way to go!" "You're an inspiration!" It feels odd. I mean I, like them, am just a hiker out for a hike. I am a hiker who feels part of something bigger when I get into the mountains. I have long since eschewed my heart rate monitor. I have grown out of that phase of hyper-athleticism, ways of reducing experiences in nature to something to measure, a means to an end, instead of an opportunity to be in and of the natural world, to realize my relative status in the scheme of things. Are these passersby urging me to not give up the fight? And if I fight hard enough, do they think I have a chance of winning? If they cheer loud enough, do they think they'll ward off the Grim Reaper?

A friend recently reported that when she asked the dermatologist about the changes in pigmentation on the back of her hands she was told in a "There, there…" tone that those spots were evidence of "sage-ing." Please, tell us like it is. Tell us in language that respects our intelligence.

Make no mistake, Bend has an amazing medical community, can legitimately claim some of the greatest practitioners and specialists anywhere. Many of us bionic Boomers are sporting artificial limbs of one sort or another, are stented, shunted, pacemaker-ed, A-, B-, C- and D-fibbed thanks to the regional health care providers. To a person, the staff in Central Oregon's medical community is dedicated, efficient and hardworking. I use these examples only to point out what is perhaps an inadvertent participation in ageism (and not limited to the world of health care). Maybe generic salutations are the best docs can do given the sheer numbers of clients. Maybe it takes up too much time, is too much of an emotional drain on doctors and staff to engage more personally. Maybe the pressure to keep up on records, to meet the unofficial quota of patients needed, precludes more personal interactions. Maybe keeping the patient at arm's-length, so to speak, is needed so doctors can focus on the process not the person, on the detective work that identifying an ailment requires as opposed to indulging the pop medicine that the patient has found online on WebMD.

Back to the annual checkup. That you know your name and have a heartbeat has been confirmed. Now the real fun begins. The nurse announces he is going to state three words and will ask you to repeat them further into the exam. Pop quiz panic syndrome sets in. You beg to recite Robert Frost's "The Road Not Taken" instead. What about the last 20 presidents? All state capitals? The three words are unrelated in sound, meaning, association. Stadium, vinegar, highway. Comb, artichoke, hem. Calculator, twine, dye. You surreptitiously write them on your palm. You know if you don't succeed your chart notes will indicate early signs of failing memory.

But take heart. There's much about memory function we don't know. With all respect to "Blursday," brain farts and impossible three-word quizzes, consider "The Doorway Effect." In studies conducted in 2011 at the University of Notre Dame it was observed that walking through doorways makes us forget things. You get up from your desk to go to the garage where your extra reams of paper are stored. Two doors later you can't remember why you came to the garage. The study concluded some forms of memory are optimized to keep information at-the-ready until their shelf life expires. Turns out, going from one room to another and walking through doorways signaled the brain to purge those memories. If the shoe fits, wear it. I plan on it.

Right now, nearly 17 percent of the population is sixty-five and older. That will climb to 22 percent by 2050. At the very least, we are an economic force, job security for many. We be Boomers! And old does not mean addled.

CHAPTER 7

Shaking the House

WHO KNEW... THE LAST WEEK OF MARCH is National Cleaning Week? Get out your brooms, stock up on elbow grease. Spring cleaning time is here! Whose idea was this? Apparently, everyone's.

Regardless of religion, culture or climate, the sweet air of spring has always prompted us to clean up our houses and our acts, to ready for the fresh starts implicit in the season. Since the eleventh century, the Iranian New Year (or Nowruz) has been observed on the March equinox and includes the practice of *khaneh tekani* or "shaking the house"—cleaning from ceiling to floor to ready for the new year. In the thirteenth century, at the moment of their frantic escape into the desert, there was no time for the Israelites to let their bread rise, only, to use current vernacular, "Grab and Go." Now, even one morsel of leavened bread (*chametz*) in the home during Passover week is prohibited out of respect of the Jews' flight from Egyptian slavery—houses vigorously scrubbed to make sure there are no overlooked crumbs. Eastern Orthodox traditions begin the first week of the spring Lenten season in March with

Clean Week during which the faithful scour their houses and, through confession, their consciences. Catholics and Protestants observe similar rituals. In the nineteenth century, before vacuum cleaners were invented, the warm and blustery winds of March were recruited to blow winter's accumulation of dust out of northern households—windows flung open wide after the long, dark, dank months of cold.

But cleaning and organizing has exceeded the bounds of seasonal, cultural, or religious practices. There's money in them thar cluttered cupboards and minds, from California Closets to meditation retreats. Marie Kondo's 2011 book, *The Life-Changing Magic of Tidying Up*, had every thirty- and forty-something throwing out baby and bath water. Her litmus? "Discard anything that doesn't spark joy." The Japanese author credits the Shinto religion as inspiration. "Cleaning and organizing things properly can be a spiritual practice in Shintoism, which is concerned with the energy or divine spirit of things and the right way to live."

Referred to as "the Marie Kondo of death," an advocate of elders getting things in order sooner rather than later is Swedish author and grandmother Margarita Magnusson, her stated age "somewhere between eighty and one hundred." Her debut book, *The Gentle Art of Swedish Death Cleaning: How to Make Your Loved Ones' Lives Easier and Your Own More Pleasant*, resulted from the painful process of sorting through forty-eight years' worth of marriage after her husband died. Building on the Swedish concept of *döstädning*, literally "death cleaning" or getting things in order before you die, Magnusson urges readers to get off their duffs and start the process at age sixty-five or before. As Michael Stevens, the founder of the Natural Mind Dharma Center in Bend, Oregon, says, "Don't put off death until the last minute."

I have definitely benefited from Margarita and Marie's advice, but caution that too much of a good cleaning-up-and-cleaning-out thing can have its downside, leaving your house or apartment feeling more like a hotel room or designer décor store. Leached of the uniqueness of those who live there, a home is reduced to a house, lacking in a different Scandinavian concept: *hygge*, the Danish and Norwegian word for coziness, contentment. Think of homemade brownies, hugs, crocheted throws, cozy slippers, picnics by the river. Personally, I like feeling (figuratively) wrapped in familiar knick-knacks, photos, books, even the errant dusty sill or cobweb. I have experienced seller's remorse after yard sales too hastily organized when a move was on the horizon. Now I am more careful. So, I confess, my garage boasts its fair share of boxes and bins, my closet is jealous of its prized oldies and not-so-goodies. Who knows? Maybe children would get to know more about their parents and, more importantly, about themselves going through old mementos and photos, slipping on a father's red wool cap with ear flaps, a mother's pair of outrageous bell-bottoms.

This time last year I had many more boxes lining my garage walls. I wish I could credit the delirium of early spring for snapping me out of my decluttering denial. But it came later. In May. That was the month Oregon was hit with the first of the many devastating forest fires of 2021. Things sorted and cleanly in place is as much about living, about survival, as it is about readying for the final farewell. It's about having that Grab and Go box ready in case of an emergency exit...at any age. I'm overcome watching Ukrainians, the young and the old, forced to flee their burning homes, with no time to wait for the bread to rise, no window to open to spring's sweet promise, no time to grab, only to go.

CHAPTER 8

More Than One Woof

IF YOU'RE PETLESS, LIVING ALONE and over (or cresting) the proverbial hill, expect to be told to get a dog either by your children, grandchildren or younger friends. Could it be the younger generation feels sorry for us fogies, equates being alone with lonely? Perhaps they don't yet appreciate their own company, a guilty pleasure for many oldies. Or maybe the get-a-dog mandate relieves the pressure they feel to spend more time with older relatives? Or do they believe old folks have nothing but time on their hands, must be colossally bored? What better to do than walk a dog three times a day, pockets stuffed with treats and plastic poop bags?

I have to interrupt this broadcast. Is there anything you can think of that's less appealing than discreetly averting your gaze as your dog struggles to deposit a stool on someone's front lawn, leaving you to obligingly pick it up? And vacations? It's easy to spend more on doggie day care than you paid for the dog. Your children's, grandchildren's and friends' enthusiasm for dogs seems to vanish when the prospect of watching Fido for a week is brought up. Actually, it doesn't matter. Your travel fund will have already been gobbled up not only by boarding fees, but also by the cost of dog insurance, drawing up a dog directive (in case you die first), vet bills, putting a fence around your yard, grooming, and sessions at dog training schools because your newly adopted best friend of man turns out to be a nonstop barker or bicycle chaser or sees everything in the house as a potential chew toy. It should come as no surprise dog ownership in the U.S. contributed 303 billion dollars to the U.S. economy in 2023.

But enough of the speculative snark. Let's hear from the bark. For Boomers, the socio-psychological benefits of having a dog sound like the best all-purpose drug on the market. If you're a Boomer and get a dog, you can look forward to feeling braver and safer, enjoying more time in nature, reaping all kinds of physical benefits (less heart disease, increased longevity, more energy, improved fitness, reduced stress). You'll find yourself more expressive and affectionate, and enjoying increased self-esteem and confidence. Add to that a resurrected sense of humor. Dogs are entertainment (check out corgis' propensity for frapping). And if your pleasure in your own company is verging on reclusive, you'll become more socially engaged with a dog at the end of a leash. People walking their dogs are always stopping to compare dog notes. Pretty soon it's a conversation, pretty soon it's community, pretty soon, if alone actually did feel a little lonely, it doesn't anymore. Plus, it's not as though those recommending old-timers get a dog don't know of what they woof. Millennials and Gen Xers are big on dog ownership.

But is it fair to have a dog in town? Herding dogs with nothing to herd? Dachshunds with no badgers to ferret? Having lived many years in remote parts of the high desert, where our working dogs had lots of space to roam, I've always felt it wrong to confine a dog to town. But this wolf-to-dog evolution has been going on fifteen thousand years. Most dogs are fine with a studio apartment. It's speculated the coevolutionary relationship between early man and wolves is why humans have thrived. According to Greger Larson, a bio-archaeologist at Oxford University,

"Remove domestication from the human species, and there's probably a couple of million of us on the planet, max. Instead, what do we have? Seven billion people, climate change, travel, innovation and everything. Domestication has influenced the entire earth. And dogs were the first. For most of human history, we're not dissimilar to any other wild primate. We're manipulating our environments, but not on a scale bigger than, say, a herd of African elephants. And then, we go into partnership with this group of wolves. They altered our relationship with the natural world."

At this stage of the wolf and human dance, I'm struck that our dog friends' job now is more important than ever...to render us more humane, remind us what it really means to be human, more in tune with the world, better able to leave it better than we found it. But what I really want to know is, when a dog stares into your eyes, does he think in English or Bark?

CHAPTER 9

Less Gloom, More Bloom

APRIL CAN BE A TRICKSTER. This year I've been April's fool, falling for the here and there glimpses of sun. On a recent rare day of warmer temperatures, I pruned and raked and fertilized until dark, certain the drear and cold were over, that spring was finally here. I bet I wasn't alone. One brief hour of sun and who didn't hurl themselves at backyards and north forties believing winter was banished until next November? Who didn't add to the inventory of cuss words getting the pull cord mower up and running, the harrow hooked up to the tractor? Who didn't walk dreamily past nursery shelves full of perennials and annuals for sale, as if lost in love, or pause to congratulate the first few crocuses pushing bravely through the soil? But waking up to more cold and gray, we all were brought abruptly back to our senses. March's lion increasingly overstays its welcome in central Oregon and April's lambswool is made not only of rain showers, but also sleet and snow.

The good news is spring will come. Regardless of age, income, or where we call home, spring has always had, and always will have, the same intoxicating effect. Renewal, rebirth, hope. Less gloom, more bloom. Earth's constancy, her willingness to show up and re-up each spring inspires the same in us.

Earth Day is aptly observed in April. It's a chance to say thank you to our hostess, to ask, "How can I help?" Here are a few suggestions from Mother Earth for Earth Day activities, hopefully with grandchildren in tow. You know them, but they bear repeating: Conserve water. Reduce energy consumption. Plant a tree. Write letters to your legislators to divest from fossil fuel investments. Pick up litter. Support a local earth-friendly organization or a national one, such as Firedrill Fridays. Plant native plants. Watch and discuss an eco-documentary. Compost. Plant pollinators. Start a community garden.

It seems to me the new three Rs are reduce, reuse, recycle. More is not better. Less is. This was underscored by the comments from Finnish citizens when they recently learned their country had been selected as the happiest in the world for the sixth year in a row. According to Penelope Colston in her April 2023 *New York Times* article, "Finns derive satisfaction from leading sustainable lives and perceive financial success as being able to identify and meet basic needs." Or, as professor Arto O. Salonen at the University of Eastern Finland, says, "...when you know what is enough, you are happy." Finns' expectations for contentment are reasonable, moderate, and if for some reason they aren't met, in the national spirit of what they call *sisu,* or "determination in the face of setbacks," they don't complain, they persevere. Less is enough.

In addition to the observation of Earth Day, April is also national poetry month. Signs of spring have the same inspiring effect on those with a pen as on those with a garden hoe. And poetry, as a form, is the maestro of doing more with less...words. Perhaps you have a favorite spring-inspired poem or quote to tape to your refrigerator door as an antidote to cold, cloudy days while you wait for gardening season. Such as this excerpt, from *It Felt Love* by Hafiz:

How
Did the rose
Ever open its heart
And give to this world
All its
Beauty?

Or this from Anais Nin: "And the day came when the risk to remain tight in a bud was more painful than the risk to blossom."

Grocery shopping on a snowy April day last week following my one day of a false spring, a bucket of daffodils caught my eye. I went home with five small bunches each with their buds tight shut. I placed them in a vase of water overnight and the next morning was miraculously greeted by a bright yellow rejoicing, a bright yellow insistence on joy, beauty, and the courage to do what, in the end, are the only things to do at any age in the face of life's seasonal challenges—channel you inner *sisu* and bloom.

CHAPTER 10

The Way Around to the North Is Still Open

THANKS TO LOTS OF SNOW AND RAIN, our rivers are singing happy, highwater songs. It's rafting season! Get out your kayaks and Catarafts! The last few years I've been invited to join five other women on a self-supported raft trip. Ten years older than my raft-mates, I relish the chance to (try to) match their stamina, dexterity and endurance on the water, to reacclimate to sleeping in a tent, to perfect campsite culinary skills, and to brave a skinny dip in cold water. So far, I haven't yet heard from the group regarding the dates for this year...

My mother grew up sailing on Buzzards Bay, a body of water off Massachusetts that boasts reliably steady winds. Just to the southwest is New Bedford, which, in the 1800s, was the greatest whaling port and richest city (per capita) in the world. Herman Melville shipped out of New Bedford, his experiences inspiring him to write *Moby Dick*. Decades later, when the idea of recreational sailing had taken hold, it was also the birthplace of the Beetle Cat, a popular gaff-rigged day sailer. My mother's idea of heaven was to guide her jaunty catboat out of the harbor into the Bay, returning hours later to drop the sail and snag the mooring, seemingly simultaneously. All this for its own fun sake, yes, but also in preparation for the highlight of her summer—the week each year she'd join three younger friends to explore the waters of Maine in a Concordia yawl.

I was home visiting my parents for the weekend. My mother and I sat talking in the living room, the French doors to the porch flung open to let in the salt-scented breezes off the Bay. "Who could it be?" she asked in response to a knock on the door. There, to her surprise, stood the owner of the yawl. She invited him in, peppering him with questions about the others on the crew, the plans for that summer's Maine adventure. Finally, he was able to get a word in. I'll never forget that moment, the look on my mother's face. Shock, disbelief, abject despair. He and the others had conferred and agreed that at her age it wasn't a good idea for her to go sailing with them. He was so sorry. His reasons, though well-intentioned, only added insult to injury: you might trip and fall, hard for you to get in and out of the dinghy...she stopped listening. This was the first time in her life she'd been disqualified from doing anything because of her age...by someone else.

We oldsters know about the societal sidelining, the invisibility, the infantilization as we advance in age. Car keys taken away. Moved out of your home at the behest of your children. Talked about in third person. It's the loss of control. Bladders are the least of it. It's one thing when you decide for yourself. It's quite another, after a long life, when decisions are made for you. Of course, if we've lost our mental or physical capacities, others have to step in. But barring that, we can jolly well captain our own ship.

We are many things. Old now happens to be one of them. Let the many, not the one, define you. As a friend used to say, "The way around to the North is still open." If we remain clever, creative and preemptive, we can find ways around obstacles to a full and purposeful life in our sixties and beyond. Ageing is unknown territory, an adventure to be embraced. Here are some big-name examples of individuals who are doing just that: At ninety-three, Clint Eastwood is heading into production for what he says might be his final film. Jerry Seinfeld has reserved Caesar's Palace for his hundredth birthday in 2054. Sir David Attenborough is ninety-seven. He remains unflagging in his attempt to wake us up to the beauty and fragility of our planet. Eighty-nine-year-old Jane Goodall and eighty-five-year-old Jane Fonda are sounding related calls to action. Closer to home, Sharon, a widow and approaching her ninth decade, still singlehandedly runs her boutique hotel in Mexico despite health setbacks that would cause most of us to turn tail and retire. With a wave of the hand, she refers to them as inconveniences. I am assisting a writer in his mid-seventies with a book about adult onset of blindness...his. The pages are filled with courage and can-do. As Carl Reiner counsels in his documentary on ageing, "If you're not in the Obit, eat breakfast." As to the raft trip this summer? No word. Perhaps it's time to read between the lines. Just in case I booked a float trip on the Snake River for this fall.

CHAPTER 11

Sun Time

HAPPY DAYLIGHT SAVINGS TIME! Sorry to say, no time has actually been saved, just shifted. We lose an hour in March to "spring forward" by adding daylight to the evening and gain an hour or "fall back" in November by adding daylight to the morning. Make sense? Not to me. But apparently it did to railroad barons, wartime presidents, and Chambers of Commerce. What they have in common is the manipulation of time for economic benefit.

Money and clock time got together long before honky-tonk singer Lefty Frizzell's compelling proposition, "If you've got the money, honey, I've got the time." To preempt federal involvement, nineteenth-century American railroad tycoons imposed the Eastern, Central, Mountain and Pacific time zones to establish predictable on-time service. The zones replaced a mishmash of local "sun times" where high noon was determined by the sun's position over their respective towns. The first U.S. law imposing DST went into effect during World War I. Although the official reason, as in Europe, was to save fuel, the U.S. Chamber of Commerce was betting more people would shop and attend outdoor sports events on sunny evenings after work. The next DST policy was enforced during World War II to reduce energy consumption, but many saw dollar signs. After that war ended many American cities, having financially benefited from longer-lasting afternoon light, stayed with the time change. The result, according to Michael Downing, author of *Spring Forward: The Annual Madness of Daylight Saving Time*, was "cities observing Daylight Saving Time surrounded by rural areas that are not, and no one can tell what time it is anywhere." To belatedly make order out of chaos, President Lyndon Johnson signed the Uniform Time Act in 1966: six months of Daylight Saving Time in the spring and six months of Standard Time in the fall. In 2005, after lobbying by barbecue manufacturers and the golf industry, DST was increased to eight months to capture the dollars consumers would spend while enjoying eight extra weeks of late afternoon tee time and burgers.

"Clock time is not what most people think it is. It was created and is frequently altered and adjusted to fit social and political purposes," says Joe Zadeh in his article, "Tyranny of Time," which appeared in *NOEMA* in 2021. To wit, Daylight Saving Time and the seven-day week were whimsically made up and, as of March 10, 2024, high noon is now high one o'clock. Zadeh states, "Like money, the clock has come to be seen as the thing it was only supposed to represent. The clock has become time itself." Indeed, time is money—to be spent or wasted. In the name of efficiency and productivity, we apply clock time to even the most natural of processes. A strict timetable for contractions, cervical dilation and delivery is now standard in U.S. hospitals. Birthing my first child in 1976, when my labor subsided the doctor quipped, "You have a union uterus! Your contractions stopped right at 5:00 p.m.!" He promptly injected me with oxytocin to get things back on schedule. Even dying doesn't get a pass. There are any number of "death clocks" online that determine everything from the total number of seconds you have left to live, to what health risks affect your life expectancy and how to average those and other data points for an even more accurate projection.

U.S. Congress is currently considering legislation to permanently impose Daylight Saving Time across the country. It looks as if money considerations will triumph even though many oppose DST. Farmers don't like it because it leaves them with less dawn light to get milk, protein and produce to market. Many citizens are fine with Standard Time as summer days get longer on their own. Doctors favor Standard Time because DST is out of sync with the natural rhythms of the body resulting in a variety of health complications. And the claims that Daylight Saving Time saves on energy consumption? Generally refuted.

Whatever the legislative decision, no sleight of time-altering hand can change what we know is the natural outcome of lives well lived. Honest acknowledgment of that most natural of cycles results in living in time with time rather than trying to bend it to economic or any other will. The grip of clock time loosens as we age. In the face of the finite, though time still flies by, it does so in a more generous and natural way...more like sun time.

Zadeh points to religious and indigenous traditions of timekeeping and to ecological clocks and calendars that have withstood the test of, guess what, time! "There are more ways to arrange and synchronize ourselves with the world around us than the abstract clock time we hold so dear."

SUMMER

Never say whoa in a horse race.
UNKNOWN

CHAPTER 12

FOMO YOLO SOLO

COVID-19 LEVELED THE PLAYING FIELD when it came to Fear of Missing Out (FOMO). After all, no one was having soirees or heading out on a camping trip or meeting at a brewery without you. No one was going to the symphony or theater or floating the river without you. During COVID, there was nothing to feel left out about.

Now that restrictions are lifting, many see the folly and insecurity of their pre-COVID FOMO ways, the unnecessary anxiety and social frenzy it caused, and are resolved not to succumb now that fun is back. We'll see. Feeling invited, seen, wanted, appreciated, up to date and up to snuff is human nature. We need validation through companionship.

As to YOLO, regardless of age, everyone charged out of lockdown waving the You Only Live Once banner, determined to make up for lost time. Forget the cost, work is overrated. After a year of having our wings clipped, "Go!" was the clarion call. Ride horses across Mongolia. Don that squirrel suit and leap off the Alps. Get that camper van, cost be damned. Because of COVID, we have to accomplish two years' worth of our bucket list in one.

And then there's SOLO. Unlike FOMO and YOLO, it's not a hip acronym. It's a condition. We now all have firsthand experience of SOLO. COVID-19 gave everyone a taste of the one-hand-clapping concept— isolated from our friends, quarantined in our houses or apartments. The poignant image of a young Black boy staring down from the window of a New York City tenement building at a world he wasn't allowed to access, to experience—he was all of us. The adult child blowing kisses to her elderly parent from outside the assisted living facility—she was all of us. When we took the first, unmasked steps toward a longed-for hug after months of distancing, we were startled to discover how emotional those reunions were. COVID created a monotone and monochrome world, a life stripped of color, sound, motion, energy and each other. Through it, we did our best. But still, isolated and alone was, well, lonely.

The older among us didn't require a worldwide pandemic to learn about solitary confinement. In 2020 the death of a partner or a divorce left 28% of boomers stranded on solo island. I say stranded because, with few exceptions, that's how people describe living alone. Remember, we're social animals. We live in a relative sense, know better who we are when we are part of a social context. Older and alone is not anyone's number one choice. Maybe you're living in the same too-big house you and your now-deceased partner shared. (Think about Airbnb-ing one of those extra rooms.) Maybe you retired just before losing a spouse and now have no travel partner, no one to share the news of the day with. (Check out trips for older travelers such as Roads Scholar, read Kent Haruf's *Our Souls at Night*, or form a caravan of camper vans and head out!) Maybe you're fearful after a divorce but living alone isn't cutting it. (Close to 15% of the population over sixty uses dating sites. The opera's not over...) Maybe dancing was your favorite activity. Maybe your grandchildren are far away. Maybe you realize that most of the world population is far worse off than you and you want to do something about it.

According to a May 2021 *60 Minutes* episode anchored by Lesley Stahl, babies born today will live until 104. The number over sixty-five in 2020? Fifty-six million. That number will be eighty million in 2040 and ninety-five million in 2060 as Boomers hit the ageing threshold, a thinly veiled way of saying a candidate for dying. Forty-two percent over sixty-five currently live alone. That climbs to fifty-eight percent for those eighty and over. Boomers are of interest, socially, politically, and economically, but to whom and why?

Let's make certain we drive the discussion about policies that affect us, rather than those who see us as in the way. There's power in oldster numbers. Boomers are a force for change, not merely an obstacle to younger generations' progress, as many would have you believe. Just when you thought all you had to think about was putting your feet up, it might be time to put your foot down, to shape the conversation about this demographic you are part of, and, while you're at it, to shape the conversation about all kinds of pressing problems that your life experience can inform.

The Central Oregon region has many different nonprofit organizations supporting arts, science, environment, families, education...and they all need you. It's well documented that isolation is, quite literally, bad for your health—so whatever you do, don't do nothing, and remember, you're not alone. Us old folks, we're in this together.

CHAPTER 13

Order and Counter Order

DECADES AGO, MY FATHER, A SEMANTICIST, published a book about dualism in Western culture titled *Order and Counter Order*. It is most definitely not what anyone would call light reading. I refer to it only because the title was invoked at my parents' fiftieth wedding anniversary. As was tradition, friends and family gathered and shared clever doggerel celebrating and roasting the couple. My father told my mother that all the times he asked her to "shut the door" to the drafty back hallway he was really saying "*Je t'adore.*" That kind of thing. It was my eldest brother who played on the title of my father's book, establishing that in my parents' relationship my scholarly father represented order and my mother, an artist, countered it, and/but the twain did meet, realizing a wonderful lifetime of love and companionship.

I don't know about you, but I like the idea of having everything in order whether my exit is precipitous or time-honored. No dirty underwear left on the floor, metaphorically speaking. Photos and Super-8 movies (remember those?) consolidated and converted to electronic files.

Last Will and Testament current, organ donor information accessible, passwords available as needed, advance directive at-the-ready. Those I hold dear will know beyond the shadow of a doubt that I cherish them. Loving and doting children and grandchildren all settled and secure. Yah, right. As they say about second marriages: "The triumph of hope over experience."

Wouldn't you agree that life is more Brownian movement than best laid plans, more musical chairs than Johnny One (perfect) Note? Unforeseen situations arise and we race to find a seat, a safe harbor, to weather the challenge *de jour* with as much imagination, information and goodwill as possible. It's just part of the deal, part of being a human on this planet. I have come to see that counter order, those enormous or small interruptions, are a given, not an option and can't be controlled or denied out of existence. Order, as it turns out, means keeping your eye on the prize while accommodating its mischievous and sometimes destructive counterpart, counter order. Aren't both needed to make the pearl? Don't both keep us thinking, adapting, stretching?

At this stage of things, I feel more a spectator of life than under the illusion I can control the outcome of anything at all—like Alice in Wonderland who remarked "curiouser and curiouser" about all that was taking place around her. Not that I came by this outlook willingly or gracefully. No. I have tried and tried to insist order on everything right along with the best of them. As they say, "How did that work for you?" Now I am intrigued to find out what will happen next, to see if putting my small oar in the water of life contributes in any way, shape or form to positive forward motion. It's a kind of proactive surrender, the acceptance of the things I cannot change and that won't go away while also remaining an exuberant participant in life.

Speaking of surrender, the idea of it recalls the notion of the beginner's mind or *Shoshin* in Zen Buddhism. An eagerness, a focus, a childlike, judgment-free willingness to try new things. What better time than in Act III? That idea of renting a flat in Paris, joining a choral group, sailing the Greek Islands? If not now, when? All those beware, take care, don't dare voices should be shown the door. As Zen Buddhist Shunryu Suzuki said, "In the beginner's mind there are many possibilities, In the expert's mind there are few." Two friends come to mind...one who took up cello later in life, participating in recitals along with the young students barely as tall as his cello bow was long. He dressed in a tuxedo, gave the recital his full attention, also giving the terrified-of-ageing parents in the audience a model for just doing it...anyway. Another who moved to Joseph, Oregon, after breaking the glass ceiling as an executive in San Francisco. She bought a small farm and, on a whim, started raising goats which led to making goat cheese which resulted in a storefront and a booth at the farmers market. What I notice is that the people over sixty-five who pull off this sort of thing first create an orderly and committed approach (the expert's mind) involving lots of planning, budgeting, and scheduling while also building in elasticity and derring do (the beginner's mind) to accommodate counter-order, bound to show up in unanticipated ways, good and bad. Ask my friend how many times her goats got out and the wonderful neighbors she met as a result. Move on opportunity or lose opportunity. Jeff Bezos has nothing on us. What is your personal equivalent of launching yourself into space?

CHAPTER 14

Play It Again, Sam

ON FATHER'S DAY, I ATTENDED an unforgettable concert. It was held, of all places, at an assisted living facility specializing in memory care. A friend of mine now resides there, a preventative decision made after months of thoughtful conversations between him and his grown children as together they weighed other options: living on his own, with family members, or in a care home. As is his wont, he has embraced his new circumstances, making more than the best of it. His humor, energy and creative generosity have already made their mark on the staff and residents at his new home.

A longtime singer, songwriter, and guitarist, he has played in bands all his life, in addition to his award-winning work in film and video. His children caught the music bug from him, all now accomplished musicians and performers in their own right. So, on this Father's Day, his family gathered in the facility's community room to honor their father and to showcase what he has always done: given to others through song. Guitars, drums, fiddles, amplifiers and microphones were set up. Rattles and tambourines were placed within close reach. The chairs filled. Additional family members and guests, come to celebrate Father's Day, added to the gaiety. Residents' canes and walkers were set to one side. Those confined to wheelchairs were rolled in. Some chatted enthusiastically while others appeared disassociated, detached from what was taking place around them. One in particular, her wheelchair situated near me, sat slumped, chin on her chest, motionless, hands resting listless on her thighs, eyes closed.

My friend positioned a stool in front of the mic, nodded in the direction of his daughter, and the band began to play with him alternately performing as lead singer or singing harmony. How comfortable he was in the saddle of song! They played rock and roll and everything in between. Beatles and Eagles, country and blues were greeted with applause and hoots of appreciation. It seemed at least one of the medley was on the personal playlist of everyone present...maybe a song that harkened back to a high school prom or one played full volume on a cross country road trip in the days of cassette tapes.

I glanced at the woman seated near me in her wheelchair. She showed no evidence of connection to herself or her surroundings, no response to the music. But then, about three quarters of the way through the concert (I don't remember the song), she lifted both her hands ever so slightly, ever so slowly, drawing them back and forth as delicately as butterfly wings in time with the drumbeat. Not a clap exactly, but close. Nothing else about her countenance had changed. But she had heard the music. It had spoken to something deep inside her.

Of the millions of Americans living in long-term care facilities, many face cognitive difficulties sometimes made worse by leaving behind their familiar surroundings, friends, and even their favorite music. Why would music matter? According to *Harvard Health*, "listening to and performing music reactivates areas of the brain associated with memory, reasoning, speech, emotion and reward." The article cites two studies, one in the United States and the other in Japan, that find that music "doesn't just help us retrieve stored memories, it also helps lay down new ones." It turns out music, especially songs, form one's formative years. They tap deep into memories not lost to dementia, bring listeners back to life, enabling them to feel like themselves again, to converse, socialize, stay present. Dr. Laura Mosqueda, director of geriatrics at the University of California, Irvine School of Medicine, states, "Music creates an 'awakening' of sorts as it reaches areas of the brain that may not be damaged by Alzheimer's and bring those pathways to the forefront."

A few years ago, I came across the documentary *Alive Inside* that follows a man named Dan Cohen who brings music to people suffering from dementia. It chronicles the astounding healing effect that music can have on behavior, mood, and quality of life. And there's more. When a stroke or brain injury has damaged the left-brain region responsible for speech, one can literally sing their way back to speaking, because singing originates in the right- (undamaged) side of the brain. First singing their thoughts, patients learn to eventually drop the melody, to speak normally. This was how former Representative Gabrielle Giffords regained her ability to speak, was able to testify to Congress only two years after a gunshot wound to her brain.

In the book *Songlines*, Bruce Chatwin recounts that Australian Aboriginals believed all things must be sung into existence. In considering the effect of music and song on our weary minds, we had better sing our cognitive connection to life into existence every single day.

CHAPTER 15

Out Late

THOSE OF US OVER SIXTY-FIVE WHO have health and stamina thank our lucky stars every day. Realizing it won't always be so results in a kind of weird frenzy...stop and smell the flowers but at the same time, go, go, go! Less superficially, with the easing of cultural, social and professional pressures during the sunset years, for some this time of life is also the final opportunity to make good on persistent and more consequential desires. The need to postpone or suppress things long dreamed of is lifted.

My parents were married in the 1930s. In a formal wedding photo, their five-year-old flower girl, dressed in an ankle-length white dress ruffled at the hem, stands shyly holding a basket of flowers. Later, as a young woman and continuing into adulthood, she successfully forged her way as an academic, eventually attaining a coveted position as a college administrator. Over the course of her professional ascent, well-intentioned friends and relatives never understood why their efforts to match her with eligible Mr. So-and-So never worked out. The answer came when she was nearly sixty. She and her female partner dared move in together after decades of closeting their feelings for one another.

One reason for their caution was the U.S. government's institution-alization of homophobia during the early years of the Cold War and the moral hysteria it sparked, to paraphrase Wikipedia. United States history classes on the 1950s typically focus on The Red Scare and McCarthyism. (Just in case it rings a 2024 campaign-year bell, the American Heritage Dictionary's definition of McCarthyism is "The political practice of pub-licizing accusations of disloyalty or subversion with insufficient regard to evidence.") But Senator Joseph McCarthy of Wisconsin was also the architect of The Lavender Scare that occurred at the same time. The Lavender Scare singled out gay men and lesbians as communist sym-pathizers and was one of the longest witch hunts in American history, a sordid campaign during Dwight D. Eisenhower's presidency to oust any and all government employees suspected of being homosexual. Thousands lost their jobs. My godfather, who served as an attorney for the federal government at that time, was one of them.

As it turns out, the egregious actions of the government back then helped ignite the LGBTQ rights movement that continues today. In 1957, Frank Kameny, a Harvard-trained astronomer, was the first to legally protest his firing during The Lavender Scare, subsequently committing himself to a lifelong fight for the rights of LGBTQ people to live authen-tically. Though there are many remaining social and political challenges, significant progress has been and is being made toward greater accep-tance. The grey and gay are taking note.

In the June 2023 issue of *InSeniors*, Amanda Combs states, "Based on Gallup polling from 2022, 7.2% older adults identify as lesbian, gay, bi-sexual, transgender...double the percentage from Gallup's 2012 study according to (the Study on Global Aging and Adult Health) and the National Resource Center on LGBTQ+ Aging. It's estimated there will be seven million LGBTQ+ people in the U.S. who are fifty and older by 2030."

Liz Maynes-Aminizade's February 2023 *New Yorker* interview with Will Shortz quotes the *New York Times* puzzle master as saying, "... I think by the time I was in my early thirties, I accepted the way I was. But a gay lifestyle wasn't something that I wanted. And I didn't need it. I have a wonderful job, lots of friends. I just live a full life. And then when I was sixty-nine, this guy came into my life who I'm crazy about, and he's crazy about me."

"More Older Women Coming Out as Lesbians," Kristin Tillotson's article (*Cape Cod Times*, January 2010) features Midwesterner Nancy Edwards for whom "the switch from straight to out lesbian came after two marriages to men. Edwards, sixty-seven, grew up in Indianapolis in the 1940s and '50s and didn't know any other way to live. 'And even if I had, in the age of McCarthyism, you didn't want to step outside the box.' After she and her second husband divorced, 'I got sober, and thought maybe my feelings for other women was from drinking too much,' she said. 'What the drinking was really about was keeping those feelings under wraps.'"

As Maynes-Aminizade concludes in her interview with Will Shortz, "... sometimes, the hardest puzzle to crack is how to love yourself."

CHAPTER 16

Assault Weapons

ON JULY 13, 2024, A TWENTY-YEAR-OLD white male was able to get his hands on a legally purchased semiautomatic AR-type rifle and nearly succeed in assassinating a United States presidential candidate. This tragedy is a call to action that includes all of us and especially those of us over sixty-five. Our experience and our perspective are critical to a reasoned and compassionate response. Before the event gets silted over with sound bites and sensationalism, before we resume our busy and distracted lives, let's contact councilors, commissioners, and legislators urging them to restrict access to these types of guns. At the national level, organizations working toward gun safety would welcome our help. The list reads like the lament it is: Giffords, Sandy Hook Promise, Brady, Everytown, Moms Demand Action. Were he to become the next President, maybe Donald Trump would now agree that accessibility of automatic weapons is something to regulate, despite dubbing himself the "best friend gun owners have ever had in the White House" at the National Rifle Association earlier this year. The more stringent the gun laws, the fewer who die by gun violence. It's that simple. In 2023, California had the strongest gun safety laws in the country and 8.7 deaths annually per one-hundred thousand. Wyoming—the weakest laws and 20.6 deaths per one-hundred thousand.

There's another weapon being recklessly brandished, one that also results in mayhem and death. In this case, thanks to our Constitution, regulation isn't an option, nor should it be. Oversight is entrusted to us as individuals. The judicious use of this potent munition is up to you and me. What am I talking about? Words. See any political spin put on this attempted assassination for what it is: at best a distraction from the real issues behind the tragedy, at worst the premeditated use of language as an assault weapon. Language misused, like guns, is powerful and dangerous. The effect is subtle, stealthy. Before we know it, conspiracy theories, distrust, fear, and paranoia are worms In our brain. MAGA's (Make America Great Again) strategically executed campaigns wielded an arsenal of violent and incendiary rhetoric, including name-calling, insults and unfounded accusations.

Words can be like bullets, yes, but they can also be powerful instruments of conciliation and forgiveness. Examples abounded after the shooting. It was so uplifting to hear expressions of compassion and concern from government and business leaders, citizens and celebrities...a joining of hands, a united team America. Pleas for calm, calls to heal the nation came from President Biden, Gabby Giffords, Nancy Pelosi, and Trump himself who said, "This is a chance to bring the whole country, even the whole world, together."

I want to believe him. I want to believe him even though this is the same man who used insulting and inflammatory language to describe immigrants, his opponents, and women; joked about a life-threatening attack on the husband of former House Speaker Nancy Pelosi; incited the attack on the Capitol in 2021; denies women their reproductive rights; lies; and sees himself above the law. I want to believe him, but I just don't.

In three-and-one-half months we will have a new President. The Republican National Convention shed some light on what a Trump presidency will look like. What's your takeaway? Will he surround himself with independent thinkers, the best in their fields? Not compromised by nepotism and cronyism? Will they be peacemakers or provocateurs? Do they embrace policies and values you identify with? How do they compare with President Biden's cabinet in view of their accomplishments over the past three years? If, like the rest of us, the President is defined by the company he keeps and is only as good as his word(s), what'll it be?

Meanwhile, I can't help but wonder if reports about how he was treated at school are true, what Thomas Matthew Crooks could have told us about the effect bullying had on his self-image and reclusive social behavior. And whether growing up in a house with twenty guns shaped his suicidal cry for help.

Comity Hour

DON'T TELL ME IF YOU DON'T WANT TO, but I bet it's true...red, blue or RFK Jr. (that's a new color on the spectrum). Aren't you feeling a little cheerier now that the political gloom and doom has lifted slightly? No one was smiling a few months ago. I mean, we, all of us, have been suffering from national smile deficiency for a long time. It's not good for our health. In some extreme cases it can cause a jaundiced appearance to the skin and hair. It can also result in what is referred to as bobble head syndrome whereby everything the jaundiced one says, those around him agree to without question.

But now, not only are we smiling, we're actually laughing! The old adage of don't take your (political) life personally seems to have sunk in. If I had to choose, I like the laughter platform far better than the never-break-a-smile one. "We're gonna go get some food—corndog?" VP pick Tim Walz asks his daughter. "I'm vegetarian," she replies. "Turkey then," Walz jokes in response.

All policies being equal, which they aren't, I just don't get the appeal of an unsmiling poor sport who resorts to calling people names if they don't kiss his, um, shoes and don't shower him with gold bathroom faucets. Give me the intelligible articulation of values and priorities served with a side of giggles any day. No more spitting nails, splitting hairs, bridge-too-far-ing or dooms-daying.

Maybe it was my internet service, but every time I searched "Jokes told by Donald Trump," what came up on my screen was, "This site can't be reached." Maybe his staff can help. Maybe they could come up with one about how crowd size matters instead of mocking democracy. "I've been indicted more times than Alphonse Capone," the felon said proudly. His jokes and laugh track have gone off the rails. Laughter has been co-opted as a sign of loyalty. And given the studies that prove humor hinges on high intelligence, Trump is decidedly unhinged.

If I were an adviser to the never-break-a-smile party, I'd suggest they go into a huddle and learn some clever wisecracks, the kind that make people laugh with one another, not at one another. As *Politico* correspondent Jeff Nussbaum wrote in April 2024, the formula at the annual White House Correspondents' Dinner is to "deliver some self-deprecating jokes, which buys the speaker the credibility to aim a few barbs at various rivals, and then conclude with a call to patriotism, bipartisanship and bonhomie." He cites a few examples: "... JFK famously sharing a 'telegram' from his wealthy and powerful father reading, 'Dear Jack: Don't buy a single vote more than is necessary. I'll be damned if I'm going to pay for a landslide.'" In 1982, Nancy Reagan, bedeviled by the scandals kicked up by her spending habits, peeked out from behind a rack of clothes and sang, to the tune of "Second Hand Rose," her version: Secondhand clothes. In 2019, John Kerry looked at his tablemate Mike Bloomberg and said, "Usually, when I'm next to someone this rich, I propose." Trump never attended the Correspondents' Dinner during his Presidency. Why? "It is impossible for you to be angry and laugh at the same time. Anger and laughter are mutually exclusive ..." according to Wayne Dyer. The frown gang is intent on stoking anger, fear and division, so no wonder laughter isn't part of the game plan. "You cannot be mad at somebody who makes you laugh—it's as simple as that." Thank you, Jay Leno.

One last suggestion that might be of interest to the no-grins team. If their fearless leader is worried about health and longevity, all the more reason to yuk it up. "Mirthful men seem to be protected against infection. And live longer," according to Tori Rodriguez in her article, "Laugh Lots, Live Longer," that appeared in a 2016 issue of *Cognition*. There are all kinds of real health benefits from laughing. So, what's the holdup? It's free. For some that might make laughing risky, one more of those free, government handout programs.

As *Saturday Night Live* decides who will best impersonate Kamala Harris, Tim Walz, JD Vance, RFK Jr., Trump and Trumper, as laughter and joy are reintroduced as an element of a solid presidential platform, as homespun, plainspoken and truthful make a comeback...whatever your persuasion, you have to admit, laughter is the best medicine for us all.

CHAPTER 18

Enough

"IN A SENSE WE ALL ALREADY know What Is To Be Done, and the real problem is navigating the grief and fear and selfishness that prevents us from ever actually putting what we all know to be true into practice."

This quote is from author Gerry Canavan's review of K.S. Robinson's latest book, *The Ministry of the Future*, a sci-fi nonfiction that outlines humans' options given occurrences worldwide. "You know what I am. I am History. Now make me good," writes Robinson.

But how? All the tragedies, the social, environmental and economic problems—it's enough. Too much heavy lifting.

To help navigate all this I offer a favorite note-to-self. When there are problems aplenty, don't drive with your high beams on...you see too much of the road ahead. Keep your lights on low. If ever there were a time for low beams, this is it...as well as for taking a breath, for stopping, listening and not to the news. Instead, seek the counsel of nature, books, friends. It's also a time to take time to sit, stock-still, every day. Call it prayer, meditation, staring off into space. When I do, unexpected happenings show up as a result.

And here they came. Starting on May 27, 2022, the first ah-ha was reading about the video Ben Beers posted online. The former marine, who spent four years in Iraq and now is the father of two, explains why, in the aftermath of the Uvalde shooting, "...I'm turning in my weapons to the Hillsboro Police Department in Oregon. Both my AR-15 and my nine-millimeter handgun. I no longer want them. I know this will not change legislation or anything to do with gun culture in America, but, hopefully, it will be a form of symbolism. Hopefully America can wake up. Because no other country has the problems that we do with gun culture and ideation and gun violence that we do. Amend the Constitution. Amend the legislation. Amend the statutes." A day later his video had been viewed two hundred thousand times. Ben Beers is a cat to copy.

Next, an email from Oregon's former poet laureate, Kim Stafford, with the gift of a poem attached, a call to words, if you will. You can find *Poems for a Cause* (and many more that will restore your faith in all things) in his masterful collection *As the Sky Begins to Change*.

A neighbor then thought to forward me the link to Lift Every Voice Oregon, where signatures are being gathered for the "Reduction of Gun Violence Act" petition, due July 1. One hundred and forty thousand names and it's on the November ballot. A few days later a college classmate sent links to Movement Voter Project to facilitate voter registration. And then a sibling, who earlier watched a Great Blue Heron land and settle by a marsh, told me beholding that moment of elegance and beauty made him realize "our task is to love the cherishable, to love the world back to health."

And last, Garrison Keillor. Before I describe the miracle he produced at Bend's Tower Theatre, please note the average age of the above-mentioned individuals is seventy. So, no, elders do not go quietly into the night. We go thoughtfully doing what we can and what we must.

Back to Garrison Keillor. He led a two-hour-plus refresher course in being curious and goofy and open and human and caring. He reminded us that in a scarier world we need our own family and community stories (not television's or YouTube's or movie theater's) more than ever. He happens to know a few. We laughed out loud, mostly at ourselves, such is his skill. We shed tears. We sang "Let Him Have Your Burden Now," and other beautiful spirituals, belted out patriotic songs we haven't stood up and sung with others in a long time. Strangers no more, we were united in laughter, song and hope.

Canavan ends his review by underscoring Robinson's point that there is in fact enough for all, and there are solutions to worldwide problems if we but have the will to enact them. "Enough is as good as a feast—or better," he says. So, okay, I'm changing my tune from enough already to enough for all.

CHAPTER 19

Chill

ON A RECENT HOT (TRIPLE-DIGIT) summer evening at Bend's Midtown Yacht Club, my friend and I were thankful for the icy-cold mist spritzed from tiny nozzles suspended above our heads. The only two at a large wooden spool table, we welcomed a middle-aged man and his two teenagers who asked if they could join us. It's one of the unique qualities of al fresco food cart courts—strangers spontaneously sharing a common table for a meal and conversation.

While his kids ran off to place dinner orders, we learned that this young (to us) man had saved enough money to leave a high-powered, non-stop, stress-inducing, sedentary job in California and move with his family to Bend. Gaining that financial freedom took its toll. He said he arrived in Central Oregon a year ago spent, out of shape, allergy-afflicted, depressed. Looking at the fit, energized man seated across from us we had to ask...what was his secret? His answer? Sitting for prolonged periods of time submerged in cold lakes and rivers, breathing through a snorkel. You got that right. His children, who had returned with plates of food, enthusiastically nodded their affirmation, followed by a go-figure shrug.

He explained that after settling in Bend and considering next steps, he stumbled across the website of Wim Hof, a Dutch extreme athlete whose systematic exposure to cold has "enabled him to control his breathing, heart rate, and blood circulation." Our inadvertent dinner guest was intrigued by these claims and started following the teachings of this proponent of icy. He did it right, going slowly, paying attention to the dos and don'ts. He told us that, no question, his brain acuity, mood, allergies, and metabolism had improved since going cold and, for his next career, he's contemplating opening a Wim Hof branch in Bend.

In recent years, cold water therapy has become popular across all age groups. The number of meetup groups at Mental Health Swims, a British nonprofit, has grown to eighty since 2019. In New England daily dunks in the winter are a thing. From the United States to the Netherlands, the popularity of New Year's Day Polar Bear Plunges has grown to the tens of thousands, including Scotland's "Loony Dook" at which thousands brave the freezing water. Participants parade through South Queensferry acting like "loonies" preceding the "dook." It's claimed a good percentage of the loonies are still inebriated from New Year's Eve celebrations and likely lost a bet.

Similar to using cold water to cure what ails is whole body cryotherapy. It involves standing in a sealed container while extremely cold air is circulated around the body. Like the Wim Hof Method, the procedure claims relief from arthritis, anxiety, depression, and improved memory function. Unlike the Wim Hof Method, cryotherapy requires an appointment and there is a charge for each session. Hof takes a more DIY approach: start with a warm shower, gradually adjust the temperature colder and colder until you can tolerate the frigid torrent for at least two minutes.

Just mention to anyone sixty and older ways to improve brain and memory function, never mind get rid of the aches and blues, and you have their/my attention. It's sobering to realize the average age of late onset Alzheimer's is sixty. Loss of hearing, living alone, both of which often accompany ageing, contribute to dementia. We're already culturally primed for the latest and greatest, the quick fix, the one and done. Add to that the sense of urgency oldsters feel to find out what will actually make sliding into home base as enjoyable as possible, and it's no wonder the greatest generations are vulnerable to the promises of Prevagen or willing to don a swimsuit when it's below freezing. But who knew the fountain of youth would be so cold!

Despite the lack of scientific evidence on cold water therapies, in my anecdotal experience the effects of a cold shower or plunge reinforce the claims. And it's a lot more fun than popping AlphaBrain or Neuriva. If staying power is any indication of irrefutable benefits, cold water has been used to improve health for centuries starting with Hippocrates in Ancient Greece. Rolling in the snow after a sauna is a Scandinavian-perfected oldie but goodie. How about when randy young men were dispatched to take a cold shower to cool their, well, jets? Now all genders are headed for the frosty to keep synapses and muscles firing.

One of my favorite hikes in the Cascades is the thirteen-mile Green Lakes Loop. The climb parallels Soda Creek until catching the Broken Top Trail to the lakes, just on time for a picnic and an icy dip before descending via the popular Green Lakes Trail back down to the parking lot. My sore feet and tired muscles are always instantly rejuvenated by the cold swim. Everything old feels new again, including me.

CHAPTER 20

Coming Alive

WHEN I WAS SIX OR SO, my grandmother, who lived with us, would entertain me by pinching the skin on the back of her eighty-year-old hand then, letting it go, telling me to count slowly until her skin lay perfectly flat again, like a wave slowly reabsorbed by the sea. I easily counted to ten. Every time.

Then it was my turn. My elastic young skin returned to normal in an instant. Not even enough time to count to one. "You see? That means I... am...old," my grandmother would declare haughtily, pausing between each word for emphasis, as though old was something I should aspire to, with its own privileges and opportunities. To me, at six, old was a game, a foreign land, and of interest, though I couldn't say why.

Earlier this month I attended my college reunion. My fifty-fifth. I hesitated before going public with that high number, considered not mentioning it at all, hoping you, reader, would guess maybe...forty-fifth? How acculturated I am, especially as a woman, to avoid revealing my age, as though it might disqualify me from...what? Living fully? When, in our sequence of birthdays, do we stop insisting, "No, I am five and three quarters, not just five." When is it we stop being eager to claim the stature an extra year promises? When, instead, do we start buying into the North American cultural hype that old is the single most undesirable stage of life? As far as I'm concerned, the shucksters have it wrong.

I was invited to offer a session on memoir writing during the reunion weekend. Those who attended, like most everyone in this chapter of life—are grateful, after years of go-go, for time to pause and reflect, whether to record anecdotal family experiences for children and grand-children to enjoy, to introduce younger generations to who their dad or grandma really was, to offer a statement of values as shaped by trial and error, or maybe pen a retrospective of a life of adventure. But it's not all about the rearview mirror.

At every reunion a memorial is held at which the names of those who died since the last gathering, in our case the fiftieth, are read aloud. Given the number of names, how many we'd lost, this reunion's ceremony was especially sobering, profoundly sad, but, in the indomitable spirit of our class of '68, was experienced as a call to do good works in the time we have left. That sentiment was discussed in the memoir workshop with all agreeing there are not only memoirs and autobiographies to be written, but also forward-thinking books as our focus sharpens, our appreciation of life intensifies, and the counterintuitive and startling sensation that as we age...we come more alive.

This appetite and energy was underscored by the topics classmates covered during panel discussions and seminars that filled the reunion schedule. Two sessions on ageing offered get-ready, get-set solutions to the legal dilemmas and emotional challenges older generations face. "Justice, USA," a new Discovery+ series filmed by classmate Marshall Goldberg, was previewed. He stated that "the experience proved to me beyond any doubt that everyone has a great story to tell if given the right chance, and that people behind bars aren't all that different from you or me." The Reverend Anne Fowler, an Episcopal priest, spoke of *Abortion Dialogues*, a documentary to be released in October that covers six years of six Pro-choice and Pro-life advocates finding, through conversation, mutual respect despite differences. The documentary film is offered as a model for difficult discussions we now face on so many fronts. "Our time together has changed all our lives and has given me a new sense of what love can mean. And I am left with a glimmer of hope for this fractured country," says Fowler. There was a seminar on AI and another on the new ways of thinking we need to accommodate as Americans. An astronomer and an epidemiologist spoke of their local climate action work. Perspectives on the current challenges in Africa, China and Ukraine/Russia were led by classmates working internationally. Remember, this is the presumed over-the-hill crowd walking these talks. What's behind, what's ahead (good or bad), it's clear this band of college cronies won't be indifferent to either. Instead, both will be met straight on.

My grandmother embraced the status of old as one to revere, to respect. To me now, old is still a game, a foreign land, and of abiding interest. Every month in this column I try to articulate why.

CHAPTER 21

Epigenetics

EVERY JULY FOR THE PAST THIRTY-SIX YEARS, the Summer Fishtrap Gathering in Joseph, Oregon, has assembled a faculty of notable writers that offers a week's worth of genre-specific workshops for registered participants. The guest authors also anchor evening readings and panel discussions open to the public. 2023's impressive lineup included the likes of Craig Childs, Debra Magpie Earling, Jamie Ford, Perrin Kerns, Anis Mojgani, Rena Priest, Kim Stafford, and Luis Urrea. No wonder nearly two hundred attendees made the trek to the Wallowa Mountains in this remote corner of northeastern Oregon.

The Summer Gathering is always theme-based and in 2023 "Generations" was the center pole. Guest authors read about pivotal incidents in the life of their family, others about wrongs to their people or culture, still others about a deceased parent finally recognized for who they were, or the belated realization that an ancestor had led a life that deserved recounting. A sense of regret, of opportunities missed, pervaded many of the presentations.

Regret is generally defined as pain or distress over something done or left undone. As a child, reading from the 1928 *Book of Common Prayer*, that notion was underscored in unison at Episcopal church every Sunday. "We have left undone those things which we ought to have done and we have done those things which we ought not to have done and there is no health in us." Curiously, there was a decline in the use of the word "regret" from the 1950s until the 2000s, at which point mentions started increasing rapidly, according to (what else) Google. Could that surge be due to the glut of Baby Boomers reaching a certain age and looking back at their lives? At family or friends neglected? Opportunities missed? Harsh words not retracted?

In her 2012 *New York Times* article, "Praise Is Fleeting, but Brickbats We Recall," Alina Tugend wrote, "My sisters and I have often marveled that the stories we tell over and over about our childhood tend to focus on what went wrong. I assumed that we were unusual in zeroing in on our negative experiences. But it turns out we're typical." Tugend references an article titled, "Bad is Stronger than Good," co-authored by Roy F. Baumeister, a professor of social psychology at Florida State University. He writes, "Bad emotions, bad parents and bad feedback have more impact than good ones. Bad impressions and bad stereotypes are quicker to form and more resistant to disconfirmation than good ones. As with many other quirks of the human psyche, there may be an evolutionary basis for this. Those who are more attuned to bad things would have been more likely to survive threats and, consequently, would have increased the probability of passing along their genes." And, by the way, that includes emotional genes.

Please welcome author Jamie Ford to the Fishtrap stage. He is the great-grandson of Nevada mining pioneer, Min Chung, who emigrated in 1865 from Hoiping, China to San Francisco, where he adopted the western name Ford, "thus confusing countless generations," quips the author. Jamie Ford's debut novel, *Hotel on the Corner of Bitter and Sweet*, spent two years on the *New York Times* bestseller list. The genesis of his latest novel, *The Many Daughters of Afong Moy*, also a bestseller, inspired his comments at Fishtrap. As the result of exploring his ancestors' responses to adversity, he turned to epigenetics (aka emotional DNA) for answers. We've likely all heard or have witnessed the manifestations of generational trauma—unfounded fears, obsessions, addictions—but Ford believes we have neglected the epigenetic evidence and power of generational joy and optimism. Yes, it takes focus and constant practice, given how tenacious the negative is, but the rewards of that effort are what the world needs now. As a newcomer to mountain biking, he offered an analogy he had apparently learned the hard way. When mountain biking, he explained, you can bet a large rock will appear in the trail. If, when moving at the speed of life, you focus on the rock, you will hit it. If you focus on the path around it, you won't.

Ford says to start with forgiving...ourselves. "Forgiveness," he says, paraphrasing Lily Tomlin,"is giving up all hope for a better past." I don't know about you, but the exquisite and elusive truth contained in that definition stops me in my tracks. Once realized, as Ford says, then a better future can unfold. What you choose to focus on is the experience you will have. So, what's not to like about choosing optimism and, thereby, scripting a joyous emotional DNA for generations to come.

FALL

Some guy said to me: 'Don't you think you're
too old to sing rock n' roll?' I said: 'You'd better
check with Mick Jagger.'

CHER

CHAPTER 22

Possible Futures

KATE BOWLER, IN HER BOOK, *No Cure for Being Human*, says, "Everybody pretends you die only once. But that's not true. You can die a thousand possible futures in the course of a...life."

I so get that, don't you? As we live, who hasn't had to die to the loss of loved ones, or a marriage, a change or loss of a job, the community of workplace friends when we retire, the loss of riches, elusive goals, of mobility, of limb, or presumed longevity, as Bowler had to do when she learned she had a terminal disease?

As I write this column I am again not venturing outside because of smoke. I am "dying" to my notion of the forests as they once were, of the bright, crisp, clear days of late summer and early fall in Central Oregon. Of all the possible futures, which will take their places?

Have you ever grabbed your binoculars and headed to the Summer Lake Wildlife Area? It's an important stop for waterfowl along the Pacific Flyway. That these wetlands are healthy is partially thanks to the work of an unsung hero: freshwater mussels. Dropping water levels this summer stranded dozens of the tiny, efficient filter feeders on the banks of the Refuge waterways where they cooked inside their shells during the recent heat wave. Cliff swallows were another casualty. Looking like giant barnacles nestled under the brow of ditch banks and rimrocks, cliff swallows' mud pellet nests turned into kilns during the prolonged fever of heat, mummifying the feathered inhabitants inside their compact cocoons.

With all due respect to Foxy Woxy, Henny Penny and acorns, I hope we can finally agree the sky really *is* falling. The planet has been tapping on our shoulders for decades and we have, for the most part, ignored its bidding. Now it's delivering well placed right hooks to our thick noggins. Things are going environmentally haywire...never mind socially, politically, and culturally. There are days I feel stopped dead in my tracks by the grief I feel for the all of it, from mussels and swallows to all human and nonhuman suffering everywhere. Do I have to die to a temperate future? Has what we chose to do versus what we neglected to do created this present? What better possible future can we align with?

Grieving is an expression of love. I know this. It is the heartfelt tribute to what has been lost and is important, necessary, healthy. But I have come to realize grief is a rest stop, not a stopping place. It is a pause before renewed commitment and action. And though adapting to actions and roads not taken is necessary, adapting is not the same as acceptance. We adapt to this new season of smoke, to wearing masks, to the presence of tent villages in our community. We adapt to the constant rat-a-tat-tat of bad news. But that doesn't mean we accept the cause of these calamities. We can fall asleep in the hammock of grief, of acceptance...or jump back into the human race.

Then what? To get my bearings, I first tell myself to keep my lights on low beam. Driving down this rough section of Life Street along with all of you, I remind myself not to look too far down the road. Focus on what's in front of me, on the "think globally, act locally" mantra.

And what does "doing" look like? It doesn't have to be a faraway thing. It can be right here. It doesn't have to be a huge thing. It could just be a hug thing. Most importantly, it doesn't have to be a tomorrow or seasonal thing, it can be now. "Every day is a gift...that's why they call it the present, y'all!" I heard that drawled by a comedian on an ad for a television sitcom. I can't remember which one. Maybe *Ted Lasso*? But I love the sentiment!

Instead of waiting for the holidays, choose a need in this present moment. Instead of waiting until December to pick the name of a family off the gaily decorated giving trees placed around town by the service clubs, seize the present moment to give. Pick a local cause and wrap it up in a donation or volunteer commitment. Let's not die to the brightest possible future, the one in which we take care of the planet and each other.

"Every day the fate of the world, the needs of the future and the unfolding of nature...are up for grabs in each of us. Every day," says James Hollis in *Prisms*. If each of us does what we can to stanch the bleeding, metaphorical swallow by swallow, mussel by mussel, we will, as Adrienne Rich said, "perversely, with no extraordinary power, reconstitute the world."

CHAPTER 23

The Race to Finish Last

MY HUSBAND AND I ORIGINALLY moved to Oregon to ranch, first north of Brothers and later along the Crooked River. One of the many things I treasured all those years was that staying fit wasn't a separate activity scheduled into the workday or weekends, rather was part and parcel of every day—irrigating and calving in the spring; moving cattle on horseback and putting up hay each summer; gathering off the high country in the fall; winters—feeding livestock. I'd put the pickup in low gear, jump out and climb onto the bed while the truck lurched driverless across the frozen meadow. Shaggy with winter coats, nose hairs lined with frost, horses and pregnant mother cows trotted along behind, vying for the hay I'd pitch to them. And too, maintaining a household, feeding ranch hands, and caring for my three toddlers who came along for every ride.

When I moved to "town," staying fit and making a living became separate activities. While my children shredded the slopes of Mt. Bachelor, I took up Nordic skiing, learned the language of *fartleks, mousaieffs,* heart rate monitors, interval and strength workouts. Training for ski races helped me maintain the level of fitness I achieved ranching. Instead of chasing cattle down the alley, I'd line up on starting lines, go hellbent, and then wait for the results calculated to the second.

Sometime in my sixties it occurred to me I was still athletic but no longer an athlete. I did all the same activities but less often competitively and discovered I didn't miss the pressure. My focus shifted from competing to, well, exercising. And now? I don't know where I read that every adult should aim for three hundred minutes of exertion each week, but I bought into it. There are many days I have to force myself out the door for a hike to reach that weekly five-hour mark. But repeating Matthew McConaughey's challenge to "Break a sweat every single day!" gets me going. Actually, anything McConaughey gets me going but that's a separate conversation!

It turns out physical fitness is a daily chore, whether working cattle or working up a sweat in a gym. A power walk, bike ride, paddle, run, round of pickleball, yoga or dance class…eighteen thousand seconds and counting! (Friends visiting joked that they couldn't live in Bend. They couldn't pass the physical.) If compromised, your physical therapist, trainer or home health assistant can be a resource for keeping you moving. Check out the options where you live or, if in Bend, the amazing array of activities at Bend Parks and Recreation. As a devotee of Alli Jorgensen's "Total Strength and Core" class, I am proud to consider myself a twice-weekly "Alli Cat." "Move it or lose it!" she declares. And that includes artificial body parts for me and for many, the result of unregulated athletic zeal in the past. We're now less nimble, less quick, pack more ounce, less bounce. Falling is enemy number one. Balance is paramount and not just for geezer jocks. And in the broadest sense, that balance is achieved by not only stretching the muscles but also the mind.

Sanjay Gupta, in his book, *Keep Sharp: Build a Better Brain at Any Age*, belabors the oft repeated litany to try new things, learn new things. In case you hadn't noticed, recipes for health and happiness, especially for oldsters, are ubiquitous. Puzzles, studying a new language, and, yes, a proper diet. "Eat Sanjay-style," Gupta says, "breakfast like a king, lunch like a prince, and dinner like a peasant," adding that what and how much we put into our bodies affects brain function as much as physical exercise. Go long on blueberries, salmon, leafy greens and almonds. Ditch the sugar.

Why all the fuss? The purpose at this point isn't to hold it together just to avoid getting dumb and friendly, rather to take seriously the race training required as members of Team Human, each of us an essential player in an age-diverse community. If possible, this is one race you don't want to finish first.

The unavoidable declension from athlete to athletic to active. Next up? I can see "fit" on the horizon and "still kicking" looming not too far beyond. And what then? Journalist Anthony Lane, reflecting on the Tokyo Olympics, opined that "the future was restored by the sight of Athing Mu, aged nineteen, who was born and raised in Trenton, New Jersey, whose parents emigrated from Sudan, and whose long, commanding stride brought her a gold medal and a new U.S. record in the eight hundred meters. Afterward, she tweeted her reaction: 'Lol, I think it's funny that we literally run so fast and just stop once we get to the line. Why stop then?'" Who knows, maybe the end is just the beginning.

CHAPTER 24

The Scarlet A and Esprit d'Escalier

OFF ON AN EARLY MORNING HIKE, a girlfriend and I encounter three younger friends of mine on the trail. Based on a lifetime of evidence, I knew my nervous anticipation of a four-way introduction was the guarantee I'd forget a name. So I defaulted to a brief if awkward, "hello" to the threesome and my hiking companion and I then continued on our way. Of course, I immediately thought of all sorts of things I could have said to include everyone, such as ask the threesome, "Do you all know Gretel?" and leave it to them to sort out.

Forgetting names when faced with making introductions I attribute to post-traumatic-introduction-syndrome, not that there is such a thing. But as a kid I was overwhelmed by all the rules and, when tested, rarely got a passing grade.

- Look the person in the eye.
- Use courteous language.
- Use names and titles.

- When introducing someone to a small group, name the group members first.
- The order of introduction is by "rank" based on considerations of age and gender.

And then there are the qualifiers. All other things being equal, the person you've known the longest should be named first. In making social introductions, men are introduced to women as a sign of respect. Rank is more important than gender in business settings. Your relatives rank higher than your friends. I mean, come on! I make my case; I've always been miserable with introductions. This is not a late-in-life issue.

Or is it? Most of us sixty-five and older would admit that worries of cognitive decline tiptoe in at moments like this. The fear is that every brain fart (forgive the vulgarity), every instance of forgetfulness is a symptom of the Scarlet A, the queen of dementia...Alzheimer's. In the U.S., it's a disease that currently affects nearly six million across all ages, four million sixty-five and older. According to Dr. Bradley Hyman, director of the Alzheimer's disease research unit at Mass General, more deaths can be attributed to Alzheimer's than to breast and prostate cancer combined.

But it's not all bad news. As Dr. Hyman pointed out during a recent presentation, there are preemptive assessments that detect proclivity for the disease and/or early evidence of it, and there are improved medications for Alzheimer's, most effective with early detection. Funding for Alzheimer's research is robust. There is even talk of a standardized test in the future.

Oldsters are inundated with suggested ways to strengthen noggin skills. Some sound draconian, some silly, others snake oily. But the latest I recently heard about, fasting two days per month, got my attention. Complementing extensive research being conducted in Europe and Australia, a study conducted by the University of California's Leonard Davis School of Gerontology and reported in the September 2022 issue of *Cell Reports*, found dietary cycles that mimic fasting appear to reduce signs of Alzheimer's in mice genetically engineered to develop the illness. "Mice that had undergone several cycles of a fasting diet had lower levels of two major hallmarks of the disease: amyloid beta–the primary driver of plaque buildup in the brain–and hyperphosphorylated tau protein, which forms tangles in the brain. They also found that brain inflammation lessened, and the fasting mice performed better on cognitive tests compared to the mice that were fed a standard diet." And get this, the fasting mice finished Wordle in two tries and could say hyperphosphorylated fast, three times! Just kidding.

There is another approach, though it has yet to be vetted by rigorous studies in highbrow medical research centers. Let's call it the "joie de vivre" technique, the French culture's penchant to give everything a classy and intriguing name that somehow makes any gaffe, frog leg, faux pas or, in this case, ailment, seem chic and desirable rather than the possible symptom of a deadly disease. Forget about the decidedly déclassé term "brain fart." Instead, let's go with "esprit d'escalier." The French define it as coming up with the perfect repartee, the exact right thing to say but, sadly, after the fact as you're headed down the metaphorical stairs (les escaliers) or the hiking trail.

To avoid after-the-fact, to get ahead of esprit d'escalier in health and in life, means leading with esprit. Stay up to date on, need I say, names, as well as recommended lifestyle changes, tests and, when necessary, medications for what ails us. In the meantime, all the things we forgot to say or didn't think to say or thought to say too late...say them now, before we descend the ultimate staircase. *Allons y*!

CHAPTER 25

I Yam What I Yam, Said the Sweet Potato

WHAT ARE YOU GOING TO BE FOR HALLOWEEN? Here's one: a dog nose and tail, a large plastic cone to attach around your neck, and you're a wounded woof to go. Or for fun, how about an exaggerated version of yourself? Gearhead, geek, helicopter (grand) parent, couch potato, bleeding-heart environmentalist or, in my case, bleeding-heart high desert rat. Then there's dressing up as the true self—but who even knows who that is? I looked it up. It's no surprise the question, "How to know who is your true self?" produced seven powerful strategies, five steps, six steps, six ways, ten questions, and a true self quiz. Apparently, it's equal parts social expectations and fear of rejection that lead us to override the still, small voice within; to compromise the soul of the poet, musician, explorer that lives inside us. But I think we all recognize that icky feeling in our gut when we compromise our essential self. Maybe taking our true self out for a trick-or-treat night would do us some good.

I spent the last two weeks traveling at the speed of five-women-of-a-certain-age per kilometer through the picturesque Dordogne region of France. France is roughly the size of Texas and, within that, the Dordogne covers roughly four thousand square miles. It's also the county of Périgord and, just to confuse things, there are four subregions within the Périgord: Périgord green (rivers and valleys), purple (wine region), black (oak and pine woods), and white (limestone plateaus). Our fearless fivesome explored some of all four. We found it to be a land of seventeen thousand-year-old prehistoric cave paintings, of ancient and modern-day troglodyte dwellings carved into cliffs, of one thousand huge towered and turreted castles, of medieval bastides or walled cities. I can see why France and England fought for one hundred years during the Middle Ages for the right to lay claim to this beautiful territory. It boasts grand rivers: Dordogne, Garonne, Vézère, Isle, and Dronne. And now, world-renown vineyards producing Bergerac, Pecharmant and seasonal aperitifs made from walnuts, chestnuts, even prunes. Thanks to Michel de Montaigne, it's the birthplace of the modern essay. This is the land of foie gras and of truffles, with dogs, not pigs, now the preferred hunter. Weekly markets fill each village with booths brimming with local crafts and fresh produce. In addition to dogs trotting purposefully ahead of their owner (whose scarf, de rigeur, is thrown jauntily over one shoulder), there's always a cat coolly surveying the hubbub from a third-floor windowsill curled next to a pot of bright red geraniums. And to complete the visual perfection, a white lace curtain gently shifts in the open window and periwinkle blue wooden shutters startle the beige limestone exterior. Greeting each new day, as townsfolk and tourists gather at local cafés, are the peals of each town's cathedral bells and the chorus of bonjours sung in a descending scale of cheer like the delicate song of the canyon wren. A French shopkeeper told me the Dordogne is a region where "the time has not passed," evident in the elegant simplicity, precision, arrested aesthetic, and mannered choreography of each day. These communities know who they are.

Yes, five women in sensible shoes. Believe you me, it was never a look I had aspired to, but here it was. Collectively, we were married, divorced, widowed or all three. Some had children and grandchildren, some neither. All together we had weathered many setbacks, produced many miracles—after seven decades it goes with the territory. Endurance athlete takes on a new meaning. Walking sticks in hand, packs on our backs, we inhaled all the French confections of food, art, and place. And we covered all sorts of topics. The one that cropped up frequently, whether floating in a *gabarre* on the Garonne or scaling the centuries-old rock steps into Chateau Les Milandes (the entertainer Josephine Baker's former residence) was that each of us was embracing and celebrating being who we are. "I yam what I yam," we chanted, and proclaimed "yamming" as one of the great opportunities of the third act.

Life asks us all to perform so many parts in this life-play. It's the blessing and curse of being in the contemporary human race: spouse, professional, parent, grandparent. But at this moment, five women in our sixties and seventies were not only taking a true vacation tooling around the French countryside, but had entered a time in our lives of taking a permanent vacation from being other than our true selves. I'd often thought, as we age, that we'd become a more and more exaggerated version of who we always were. I used to think that was a bad thing, that we were acting really old when really, we've stopped acting. This Halloween let's all be what we yam.

CHAPTER 26

Go Ask Alice

IF CHANGE IS THE ONLY CONSTANT, WHY is it so hard to change one's mind about things? Witness the ill effects inflexible thinking is having on many aspects of our society.

But sometimes, some special times, taken separately or together, compassion, modern research and aboriginal wisdom prevail, resulting in change that is for the good of the whole.

The health benefits of standard, over-the-grocery-counter mushrooms are well known. They're a rich, low-calorie source of fiber, protein, antioxidants, vitamin D, zinc, and are an anti-inflammatory. Mushroom clubs, including in Central Oregon, are showing up everywhere, as mushroom hunters search for porcini, chanterelles and truffles. No special legislation required for these hunter gatherers. That's not the case for psychedelic varieties.

As a child, Lewis Carroll's dreamscape masterpiece, *Alice In Wonderland*, was my first encounter with the notion that a mushroom was more than sautéed garnish for red meat or a healthy addition to salad. With the hookah-smoking Caterpillar in the role of what would now be referred to as a "trip sitter" to monitor her experience, Alice nibbled opposite sides of a mushroom, one making her taller, the other—smaller. (She ultimately settled on her original height, interpreted by some to be Lewis Carroll's way of encouraging young people to accept themselves just as they are.) Grace Slick and her band Jefferson Airplane co-opted Alice's mushroom adventures in their 1967 song, "White Rabbit," to extoll LSD use:

Go ask Alice

When she's ten-feet tall

And if you go chasing rabbits

And you know you're going to fall

Tell 'em a hookah-smoking caterpillar

Has given you the call

Call Alice

Those were the early Boomer days of Vietnam War protests, freewheeling counter-culture movements, Woodstock, and lots of experimentation with psychedelics. Alarmed by the social upheaval and what then-President Richard Nixon considered rampant LSD use by young Americans, he instigated the War on Drugs in the mid-60s. In 1970, Congress passed the Controlled Substance Act, effectively halting research on the health benefits of psychedelic mushrooms.

But fifty years later psilocybin studies are back. In 2018, the U.S. Food and Drug Administration proclaimed psilocybin a breakthrough therapy in treating severe depression, a designation the agency applies to drugs that demonstrate improvement over existing treatments. In 2021, the U.S. federal government finally re-entered the psilocybin research game, having left the funding during the hiatus to private institutions, including a 1990s John Hopkins study that identified the benefits of psilocybin when used to treat depression, chronic pain, addiction and anxiety. In 2020, Oregon voters approved a ballot measure to initiate a regulatory and licensing framework that, beginning in 2023, allows patients to take psilocybin under supervision. Oregon is the first state to do so. According to a 2020 Pew Trust survey, "the Connecticut legislature has started the process toward legalizing centers in which veterans and first responders could be administered psilocybin...Texas, Utah and Washington State have set up task forces or funded research into the medical use of psilocybin. Maryland has created a $1 million fund to study alternative treatments, including psychedelics, for PTSD or traumatic brain injury, and to pay for such treatments for veterans. Ballot initiatives that would legalize psilocybin are underway in Colorado and California. Ann Arbor, Michigan; Denver; Oakland, California; and Seattle, have passed measures that essentially decriminalize psilocybin mushrooms... ." We're in what some refer to as the "Psychedelic Renaissance," a bit ironic in that indigenous populations around the world have recognized the beneficial effects of psychedelics for hundreds of years. It's not the first time "modern" culture is late to the plant party.

In his book, *How to Change Your Mind: What the New Science of Psychedelics Teaches Us About Consciousness, Dying, Addiction, Depression, and Transcendence*, author Michael Pollan examines LSD, psilocybin, Ayahuasca and other compounds for "their potential to relieve several kinds of mental distress, including depression, anxiety, and addiction. "Several of the scientists I profile," he says, "are convinced psychedelics could revolutionize mental healthcare and our understanding of the mind." All this sounds like a reason for anyone suffering chronic pain, stress, or mental health challenges to celebrate!

But not so Oregon fast. Just as with the 2016 process of cannabis legislation, Oregon's psylocibin measure gives counties the ability to opt-out. Many that did in 2016 are doing so again...although it should be noted the 2016 naysayers have since relaxed their opposition to cannabis and, thank you very much, are profiting from their change of mind. So how about a change of mind on this issue as well? How about clearing the way for regulated and supervised psilocybin uniformly available to help all Oregonians, young and old, in health- and life-enhancing ways we only just begin to understand? As Michael Pollan says, "This book has taken me places I've never been—indeed, places I didn't know existed."

CHAPTER 27

Left Right Center

HAVE YOU DISCOVERED THIS ZANY, too-much-fun game? Everyone brings one dollar. Chips work, too. Three dice, each inscribed with L, R, C and a dot. Gambling-lite. It requires no skill other than coming up with your own surefire incantations to guarantee a winning roll, e.g. "Show me that you know me!" or your version of the pre-serve sequence perfected by Spain's tennis wonder, Rafael Nadal, hopefully minus the crotch grab. Isn't it astounding how we believe we are in control of outcomes, the course of fate? Yoo hoo! Our lot is to embrace, make the best of what we get, offer our best efforts, accept the outcome, give thanks, be good sports, make lemonade...all that. But back to Left, Right, Center. You want to roll the single dot. Then you don't have to pass your dollar to the person on the right or the left, or, worst of all, permanently sacrifice it to the growing jackpot in the center. Eventually, the winner takes all. They don't have to, though. They could, instead, redistribute the dollars, all or some, so the game can go on, the fun can continue. Hoard or pay forward. And how about the losers? Accept? Protest? Leave the game? Demand a rerun?

As we gather for our simple to extravagant versions of Thanksgiving with strangers-to-be-friends, BFF's, family, kin, don't just leave your shoes at the door, leave the political left and right of you there too, please. If you can, stay centered in family, focused on what matters, like saying thank you. Family and giving thanks are church. Politics are state. Younger generations at the table are watching us olders for signs of wise elders.

In addition to the aptness of the name of Left, Right, Center in the wake of the midterms, my rah, rah comments are also inspired by a November 9, 2022, post by American historian Heather Cox Richardson. She writes, "It puts me in mind of what poet Walt Whitman wrote about the momentous election of 1884. In that year the Republican Party had become so extremist that many of its members, disparagingly called "Mugwumps" by party loyalists, jumped ship to vote for a reformer, Democrat Grover Cleveland. It was a chaotic and consequential election, for it showed those Republicans who stayed with the party that they must moderate their stances or become a permanent minority. Younger Republicans like Henry Cabot Lodge of Massachusetts, Robert La Follette of Wisconsin, and Theodore Roosevelt of New York took notice and turned their party back toward its roots, protecting the rights of individuals rather than of corporations. By the end of the century, they had captured the imagination of the nation...but on Election Day, 1884, all anyone could know was that there were currents and crosscurrents. What would come from any of them would not be clear for another decade or more."

She then underscores that, given how tense things were in that 1884 election, the miracle was that voting took place at all, the right to choose our lawmakers was exercised. She closes with Walt Whitman's words, an anthem really, written in an English of old.

"If I should need to name, O Western World, your powerfulest scene and show,
'Twould not be you, Niagara—nor you, ye limitless prairies—nor your huge rifts
   of canyons, Colorado,

*Nor you, Yosemite—nor Yellowstone, with all its spasmic geyser-loops ascending
to the skies, appearing and disappearing,*
*Nor Oregon's white cones—nor Huron's belt of mighty lakes—nor Mississippi's
stream:*
*—This seething hemisphere's humanity, as now, I'd name—the still small voice
vibrating—America's choosing day,*
*(The heart of it not in the chosen—the act itself the main, the quadriennial
choosing,)*
*The stretch of North and South arous'd—sea-board and inland—Texas to
Maine—the Prairie States—Vermont, Virginia, California,*
The final ballot-shower from East to West—the paradox and conflict,
The countless snow-flakes falling—(a swordless conflict,
*Yet more than all Rome's wars of old, or modern Napoleon's:) the peaceful
choice of all,*
Or good or ill humanity—welcoming the darker odds, the dross:
*—Foams and ferments the wine? It serves to purify—while the heart pants, life
glows:*
These stormy gusts and winds waft precious ships,
Swell'd Washington's, Jefferson's, Lincoln's sails."
I have voted in fifteen presidential elections and countless midterms,
placed my ballot in the box accompanied by the most fervent of incantations. Even so, often the results weren't what I wanted. What's as good is
how reassuring and invigorating it is to see that the warp and woof holds
and hold, how the fabric retains its core strength despite, despite. I am
thankful to be a participant in this grand experiment called democracy.
It's asking each of us to "show me that you know me." We just did and we
will again, again.

CHAPTER 28

Falling Toward Spring

TAKING A SPILL WASN'T A MEDICAL RED FLAG when first learning to ride a two-wheel bike or, at thirty, cartwheeling down the ski slope leaving a trail of goggles and skis. So Boomers, when you commit a young person's type of fall, don't admit to your doc you tripped on a root while on a September hike. If you do, you'll be subjected to an ageist double standard, and forever more be considered a "fall risk."

Having said, it is true that the healing response after a certain age is slower, so best not to imitate Superwoman or Spider-man. And there's good reason to listen to internists' practical advice, like never hike with your hands in your pockets. Kind of like, never squat with your spurs on. They might prescribe poles, a walking stick, a cane, even an all-terrain walker when frequent falling is an issue. And then there's the fact that once you're over sixty-five, falls can signal that uninvited guests are crashing your life's party. Physical and mental conditions we never dreamt we were candidates for are part of the initiation into this venerated club called old age. Many of those conditions are signaled by stumbles. So, in a practical sense, the proactive diligence of medical professionals is worth its weight in gold.

But when the cause of the falls, literally or figuratively speaking, can't be fixed and won't go away, something other than practical solutions is needed. They're hard to embrace, especially given our cultural programming to figure things out, to make a plan and execute it, so all will be well. But some situations (whether physical, emotional, financial, or circumstantial) just do not respond to logical problem solving. Then the only available "plan" is an illogical one: surrender. To paraphrase Phillip Simmons (1957-2002), author of *Learning to Fall*, life is not a problem to be solved but a mystery to embrace.

For the doers and solvers that we are, surrender sounds scary or, at the very least, not practical, nonsensical—akin to letting go of the steering wheel while the car is moving. But as I say goodbye to friends facing death with extraordinary calm, dignity and courage, as I spend time with age-mates living creatively and mightily with physical and medical challenges, as I consider my own seven decades and the world around me, Simmons' words ring true. "At one time or another, each of us confronts an experience so powerful, bewildering, joyous, or terrifying that all our efforts to see it as a 'problem' are futile. Each of us is brought to the cliff's edge. At such moments we can either back away in bitterness or confusion, or leap forward into mystery." Diagnosed with ALS, or Lou Gehrig's disease, at age thirty-five, Simmons states that his book's central theme is a paradox: "In the act of letting go of our lives, we return more fully to them."

Think of all the ways we can fall—out, over, or through. We can fall back (Hello, Daylight Saving Time in November!), fall for a joke, fall in love. And while we're in the midst of the fall, we can't possibly know the outcome. Like life itself. Simmons encourages us to, "Find victory in the falling, the not knowing." As to the inscrutability of life, to the unanswered questions that plague us, he reminds all we can do is love and be kind. It's what Jesuit priest and founder of Homeboy Industries, Gregory Boyle, calls radical forgiveness of self and other. It's hard work but maybe the only work.

Rainier Maria Rilke, writing in the 1900s to a young protégé in *Letters to a Young Poet*, penned this antidote to life's unanswered questions: "I want to beg you, as much as I can, dear sir, to be patient toward all that is unsolved in your heart and to try to love the questions themselves like locked rooms and like books that are written in a very foreign tongue. Do not now seek the answers, which cannot be given you because you would not be able to live them. And the point is, to live everything. Live the questions now. Perhaps you will then gradually, without noticing it, live along some distant day into the answer."

September marks the beginning of another cycle of dying to life, of dying and rebirth, in this eons-old tumbling act. If you're a leaf falling from a tree in the autumn, what are you falling toward? I'd say spring. I'd say toward living everything.

CHAPTER 29

What a Way to Go

I'M NOT ONE OF THOSE WHO CAN chop parsley and put a last-minute sear on the steak while simultaneously greeting guests. I try to get party preparations done in advance to avoid last-minute fussing. Once I've done what I can and guests start to arrive, I surrender to the will of the occasion, to its alchemical (or lack of) success. *Que será, será.*

Doing all we can with the best of intentions, then saying goodbye to any fixed notion of how it's going to turn out, is a lesson that life teaches. So, too, the contemplation of death. Though the Grim Reaper isn't generally characterized as welcome or pleasant company, readying for its arrival in advance renders it less of a surprise, less the party crasher, and provides the chance to learn from it while we're still kicking.

It's recommended to begin preparations while you still have the mental, physical and legal capacity to document your end-of-life wishes. Note to self: That would be now! DeathwithDignity.org is one of many resources that helps individuals plan for the last hurrah. The website includes a Life File Checklist prescribing what to do, from data to advanced directives, from memorial to burial. If you find yourself procrastinating, there are organizations that can help, such as Bend's Peaceful Presence Project. Their highly skilled doulas assist with the emotional as well as the practical side of things. You can also take care of the planning yourself.

For the DIY-ers, writing your own obituary ahead of time is the rare opportunity to have, well, the last word. It's uncanny how differently you see yourself when observed from the third person, from the impassionate distance of he or she, never mind the reality check summing up one's life in two hundred words provides, and the realization there really is no time to waste.

Funerals and memorials also allow for before-the-fact participation. At a recent celebration of life I attended, the deceased had curated the slide show, given the speakers time limits and topics, created a playlist for the event, and even provided all in attendance with a to-go list of aphorisms he'd collected over the course of a rich life. My favorite: "Nothing good happens after midnight." His death-defying energy and unique signature suffused all aspects of the memorial.

Speaking of signatures, signing off on an advance directive becomes more complex as new choices about where, when and how to exit become available. The desire to be the architect of one's waning days has increased in proportion to medical advances that artificially prolong life. There are now at least ten states, including Oregon, that offer Death with Dignity. One courageous and elegant implementation of this process was shared by Oregon's accomplished fiction writer Cai Emmons in her online piece, "Wrapping Up a Life." After years of living with ALS, she orchestrated her death in 2023. As an alternative, Switzerland, Canada, Belgium and The Netherlands offer assisted death services. In a November 2021 article in *The Guardian*, titled, "A trip to Switzerland in search of a good death," Charlotte Naughton movingly recounts her aunt's decision to go to a clinic near Basel to die intentionally. These are both must reads.

And then the question, what to do with the body that isn't the Aunt-Edna-strapped-to-the-roof-of-the-station-wagon" solution? As concerns about the toxicity of the cremation process increase, other options, such as aquamation, are becoming more popular. In both cases, an urn of remains is provided to survivors to distribute in the location specified (hopefully) by the deceased. Also for environmental reasons, burial in a non-biodegradable coffin is being supplanted by a green burial, also known as human composting, using a biodegradable casket or shroud. Some are enhancing biodegradation by selecting the "mushroom burial suit" infused with spores to hasten the process and filter all toxins from the decomposing body. And what about anatomical donation? At his death, my beloved father was, according to his wishes, whisked away to a nearby medical school in a refrigerated van. For my money, both green burial and body donation strike me as paying it forward in some funky afterlife kind of way.

My irreverent tone notwithstanding, I tremble in the face of the mystery, of the vast unknown. But whether death is seen as eternal oblivion or sure resurrection, being as ready as possible allows us to enjoy the party, to surrender to *que será, será*. On her death bed, my friend's aunt, distracted by the commotion in the hospital room made by grieving family members, called her favorite niece over to her and whispered, "Please, Jane, tell them all to leave. I have never died before and I want to enjoy it."

CHAPTER 30

Sound Off

WHAT ARE YOUR AUTUMN MEMORIES and traditions? Making favorite soup recipes? Taking in a film festival? Bagging a deer, antelope or elk? Tailgating with friends at a football game? Fall has arrived. What a beauty, with Indian Summer prolonging outdoor playtime against a multi-colored display of foliage. It's hard for me to imagine living somewhere that doesn't have distinct seasons. As the temperatures cool, it's a "hygge" time of year, as the Danish would say, a time of cozy, of quiet, before the hullabaloo of the holidays.

But quiet, as it turns out, is a more and more precious commodity. If the ambient sounds in your place of work are a distraction (HVAC, Muzak, intercom), if the sounds in your apartment complex or neighborhood (leaf blowers, revelers, sports cars' vroom) are a source of frustration, you're not alone. Raise your hand if you can hear traffic from your house. Too much of anything is not good for us.

The U.S. Environmental Protection Agency has set a standard for a twenty-hour exposure limit for noise levels at 70 dBA—measured in decibel units (dB) and A-weighted (dBA) to adjust for human hearing. Some OSHA sites say 80 dBA spanning an eight-hour period for workers is acceptable while others say 90 is tolerable. The urban residential ideal is 45 to 55 dBA but is more and more difficult to achieve given how noisy we have become. The soundproofing of houses under construction is trending. Creating noise-absorbing green space between new developments and busy roads is a popular notion, but what booming community is willing to give up space for housing given the fill-in and build-up-not-out pressure placed on builders by municipalities? Unwanted residential sounds are masked by white noise piped into rooms, strategically placed automated water features outside, or deflected by high, impervious walls. To put noise pollution in perspective, a vacuum cleaner, leaf blower or hair dryer produce a noise level of around 80 to 90 dBA. Normal conversation—60. Distant traffic is 70 to 75. Arrowhead Stadium in Kansas City, Missouri, registered 142.2 at a game in 2014. That's the equivalent of standing next to a jet engine at takeoff. Chronic exposure to unsafe levels of sound has been shown to be a primary cause of deafness in older generations, never mind a host of stress-related issues at all ages.

We have been fed such a steady diet of distracting noise, we can feel disoriented without it. I shopped in Natural Grocers recently and was initially thrown by the absence of piped-in music, of special deals announced over the intercom, of the artificially created sense of cheer and hubbub. But I then realized what a pleasure it was to hear only the unadorned sounds of people shopping. In some respects, we've become dependent on noise, get nervous when it's too silent. No wonder we can't hear ourselves think. The popular reaction to this realization has been a growing appetite for silence and learning how to be comfortable with it. Activities like forest and moon bathing or vacationing in remote resorts predicated on, and charging plenty for, helping their clients unplug and get quiet are proliferating.

What these noise problems have in common are the ever-rising din of man-made sounds. What the solutions have in common are soul-nurturing natural soundscapes. In the name of progress, we are unwittingly overwhelming the sounds of Nature. Nobody knows this better than Emmy-winning acoustic ecologist Gordon Hempton. His documentary (and book by the same name) *One Square Inch of Silence* recounts Hempton's search for locations where the chirps, yowls, hoots and splashes of nature are the sole sounds. He was able to identify only twelve locations remaining in the United States where his breathing was the solitary measurable noise. Of those he divulges just three, keenly aware of mankind's propensity to love to death the very things that are critical to holistic survival. One is the Hoh Rain Forest in his home state of Washington. "Anonymity," says Hempton, "becomes the only viable protection." Astoundingly, he discovers that one preserved square inch of wildlands' intricate cacophony affects, by association, one thousand square miles.

It's no secret Nature's symphony brings us more in tune, that clanging towns render us off-key. "Natural silence is our nation's fastest-disappearing resource," warns Hempton. Before International Noise Awareness Day on April 25, let's give one inch of high desert over to noise protection and watch it take not one, but one thousand square miles.

CHAPTER 31

Old Glory and Dhar

ON VETERANS DAY THIS YEAR nearly three thousand flags lined the main streets of towns across Central Oregon. Redmond, aka Flag City USA, was in the lead with one thousand six hundred stars and stripes placed by volunteers hours before that city's parade began. Throughout the region, the best of hometown parade pageantry was on full display: high school bands, Girl and Boy Scouts, the Oregon Youth Challenge Color Guard, rodeo queens and their courts, military vehicles, Mountain View High School's Navy National Defense Cadet Corps, and the veterans themselves. In Madras, the Black Bear Diner offered a free meal to all who served in the armed forces. Burns High School hosted a Veterans Assembly that included tributes along with a tasty brunch.

Veterans Day was originally Armistice Day to commemorate the truce between the allied forces and Germany signed at the eleventh hour of the eleventh day of the eleventh month of 1918 and leading to the end of World War I. In 1914, Author H.G. Wells dubbed WWI "the war to end all wars." If only, if only he'd been right. But despite, or maybe because of, the Ukraine-Russia and Israel-Palestine conflicts and other battles across the globe, on Saturday, November 11, 2023, Veteran's Day commemorations took place throughout the United States with the American flag front and center.

It's a flag that has long stood for a democracy founded on respect, loyalty and reason, on loving one's neighbor. But in recent years older veterans of war and life have seen Old Glory rendered less a symbol of patriotism, the emblem of team America, and more a political symbol as defined by one faction or another. From my Baby Boomer perspective, a term coined to describe the increase in birth rate after World War II, I can't help but feel the freedoms we cherish, that veterans have given their lives to protect, are in real jeopardy given the divisions among our own ranks.

I recently made good on a longstanding promise to myself: a trip to the small nation of Bhutan. My dream of visiting this tiny country nestled at the foot of the towering Himalayas was fueled by images of breathtaking natural beauty as well as Bhutan's reputation as the happiest country in the world. In 2008 the country established goodwill as a policy, adopting Gross National Happiness as a "development indicator, formalizing the country's belief that happiness is a core responsibility of government." I kid you not. "It provided the world with proof-of-concept for moving beyond GDP [Gross Domestic Product] measurement and taking a holistic view of social development," according to an article co-authored by Asian Development Bank economist Milan Thomas and Yangchen Rinzin, a fellow at Bhutan's Centre for Gross National Happiness Studies. What does that look like on a day-to-day basis? Compassion of one individual for the other, lack of self-aggrandizement, respect and caring. This is not an exaggeration.

The country's national flag, yellow and red bicolor with a dragon in the center, is displayed in Bhutan's cities, but stealing the show are the colorful Bhutanese prayer flags (dhar). They are everywhere. They dance from lines strung atop the tallest mountains, across the deepest chasms, and from towering Cypress trees. The flags festoon the steepest cliffs, surround ornate temples and stupas, and are an integral feature at the Buddhist monasteries located throughout the country. The belief is by hanging the flags, the prayers they carry for happiness and freedom from suffering are released far and wide. I returned from this trip truly inspired by a culture predicated on the good of all, a concept that shouldn't feel so foreign, so unusual.

Sometimes it takes getting out of Dodge to shake loose a new perspective. Distance or destination needn't be the determining factor. After a high desert out-and-back or a hike into the Cascades, I always see and feel more fully when I return to the hubbub of town. Admittedly on this trip I traveled crazy far to be reminded that personal happiness depends on the happiness of others and to witness firsthand that happiness as a governmental policy is possible.

I can't help but wonder what would happen if, instead of the flags we fly to noisily proclaim our divisive political positions, we respectfully flew giant prayer flags from our vehicles, releasing to the winds our wishes for mutual caring, the end of suffering, for peace at home and abroad. My bet is, if we did, we'd move mountains the size of the Himalayas on the way to victory in the campaign for compassion.

CHAPTER 32

Existence Value

I RECENTLY HAD THE PLEASURE of attending a gala for the Friends of the Malheur National Wildlife Refuge. A small but mighty nonprofit promoting "conservation and appreciation of natural and cultural resources...through education, outreach, advocacy, and on-the-ground stewardship," its territory includes nearly one hundred and ninety thousand acres of critical wildlife habitat. The gathering coincided with the birthday of an individual considered the founder of the Friends of Malheur and, by most in the room, also credited with starting the Oregon Natural Desert Association, Bend's Environmental Center and the Central Oregon chapter of Great Old Broads for Wilderness. When it was her turn to speak, she skipped to the podium smiling but shaking her head, hands in the air in protest as though stopping the praise in its tracks. She proceeded to purposefully, with humor and humility, refute all the recognition, shrugging it off, placing the shawl of acclaim around the shoulders of deserving others in the room.

A concept I had never heard of was introduced to me recently: "existence value." Environmentally speaking, it refers to the "value" of knowing that a particular species, habitat or ecosystem does and will continue to exist because it is being protected, like the Malheur Refuge. The existence value of an environmental resource, also referred to as non-use or passive value, is, by definition, "free of any use that the valuer may make of a particular resource." It refers to the value of benefits derived from the mere existence of a natural asset, the knowledge and trust that Crater Lake, for example, exists pretty much unfettered by human activity. A tree, for instance, can be valued in a number of ways: use (as lumber), option (things that it could be used for), or existence (simply being there). Saving the best for last, it's simply being there we're talking about here.

Each of the organizations the guest of honor was credited with founding works to preserve the Great Basin desert in different ways. To the extent that awareness of what and why those organizations matter increases, their existence value also increases and, as a result, contributions to make sure they stay protected increase. Even though we may not visit these natural resources, the mere knowledge of their safeguarded existence provides a sense of reassurance, a sense that things are right in the world.

But does this term refer only to an environmental resource? Halloween will be here soon. I can imagine children going up and down the streets in the New England town I am from, a town essentially frozen in time, which, in my twenties, was a good reason to leave. But I now find I am reassured by the knowledge that younger generations of the families I grew up with are putting gardens to bed, tying off onion tops, gathering corn stalks to decorate front porches, carving pumpkins, just as we did. Now that change seems more of a constant than ever, that my hometown stubbornly persists as its unchanging self is a source of contentment. Does the knowledge that treasured traditions live on have existence value? What about memories? And what about, say, museums that trigger a memory of an existing natural resource which then activates our appreciation of that resource's existence? Would that be double existence value?

The individual honored at the gala was Alice Elshoff. It was her nine-tieth birthday. I maintain individuals like Alice Elshoff have existence value. The high desert would wholeheartedly agree. Alice isn't the desert itself, but her commitment both complements and mirrors its value, the absolute necessity of its existence as a prerequisite to our own. That people like Alice persevere has incalculable inspiration value. And if inspiration spurs action for the good of the planet, then ...well, you see all the fun places this can go.

Of course, we can write a check and bask in the knowledge that our generosity has helped protect a fishery or orphanage or butterfly. But that the term "existence value" exists at all depends on those who are on the frontlines, forwarding the conservancy and humanitarian causes we support—like Alice, who headed out on a work project at the Refuge only days after the tribute dinner..Below is an excerpt from a poem I wrote for Alice that evening:

> *Here's to our high desert's queen Mum,*
> *our Sedna of the sagebrush ocean.*
> *May feather, branch, paw, hoof, hand,*
> *and blossom daily join*
> *in a circle dance of thanks*
> *to you, Alice, angel and warrior,*
> *the high desert's curandera.*

WINTER

Without an ever-present sense of death, life is insipid.
You might as well live on the whites of eggs.

MURIEL SPARK

CHAPTER 33

Just One Mistletoe Minute!

I'M A SOFT TOUCH WHEN IT comes to the finals of any team compe-
tition. Good luck picking what to watch over the holidays! Christmas
Day–all about the NBA. Boxing Day is devoted to that *other* kind of football. Don't forget the New Year's Six! Whichever sport, it doesn't take a
rocket scientist to know players stand a better chance of winning if they
function as a team. Armed with the written rules of the game as well as
the unwritten ones of good sportsmanship, the job of creating and sus-
taining a winning team falls to the coach.

Speaking of teams and coaches, call me a dreamer, but here's my
Holiday wish: that for just one mistletoe minute everyone in the United
States imagines themselves as members of one team. Playing different
positions, sure, but part of one Team USA, a team that plays by the
Constitutional rules and collaborates on sea to shining sea solutions that
address challenging sea to shining sea problems. And as for coaches—
until the 1980s every high school had a dedicated coach to teach these
team concepts, to lay the foundations of all-for-one. That would be the

civics teachers. They taught not just politics and government but also the responsibilities of being a citizen, the importance of community service, of giving back. Assignments might include attending a city council or school board meeting or writing letters to the editor. Civics taught the importance of a don't-quit attitude of problem solving coupled with a passion for serving others, of taking one for the team (as Will Nunn of Culver, Oregon, underscored in a must-read guest column in Bend's *The Bulletin*).

Civics is on life support in this country. Recent surveys show civics instruction, if it exists at all, is at best a half-year requirement. In 2016 not one state included experiential learning in its civics curriculum; instead only the thin gruel of memorizing political and government organizational structures. Currently, the closest thing in Oregon is the Kid Governor Program for fifth graders, originally created in Connecticut and adopted in 2017 by then Oregon Secretary of State Dennis Richardson. Subsequent Secretaries of State have renewed the commitment. Nonprofits, such as the Classroom Law Project and YMCA's Youth in Government, help fill the civics gap, but these programs often have a cost attached and are chiefly available in urban areas. The good news is, after numerous legislative attempts to reinstate civics, the 2021 Oregon legislature passed the Civics Education Act requiring one semester of civics to graduate from high school, effective 2025. Representative Paul Evans, D-Monmouth, who has worked to pass civics requirements for Oregon students since 2014, celebrated the bill's passage "...this landmark bill will give the next generations of Oregonians the knowledge and tools they need to lead."

In 2016, the Annenberg Public Policy Center found only one quarter of Americans could name all three branches of government, never mind the purpose of the Bill of Rights. Wouldn't you agree there's a direct correlation between the lack of high school civics and why we Americans are increasingly unaware of the basic functions of our government; between the lack of civics education and why we Americans are cannibalizing our own home team, veering away from all-for-one to a house divided?.Whether a sports team or a nation, we know how that story ends and it's not pretty.

Boomerdom spans from 1946 until 1964 with Boomers accounting for roughly 22% of the current U.S. population. Plenty of us served in the military or in other ways, such as in the Peace Corps (that was my pick) or Vista, the domestic version at the time and now one of the AmeriCorps programs. I was in college during the Vietnam War when students called for an overhaul of the Selective Service Act to make approved forms of civilian service count as a legitimate alternative to military service. In many countries some national service, either civilian or military, is required. Maybe it's an idea whose time has come, a way to realize commitment to country, to learn and practice critically important civics lessons.

"Thank you for your service," the ticket agent says to veterans or those currently serving in the military. What if, when the attendant called for those who have served to board their flight early, we all could stand up? What if all of us were eligible for the Veterans Day parade...floats proclaiming affiliation to both military and civilian service? So okay, maybe more than one wish: that civics be reinstated in high schools everywhere, that military and civilian service to country be recognized and, in the meantime, that we all do our level best to be team players. Call me a dreamer.

CHAPTER 34

Credo

SO, NEW YEAR'S RESOLUTIONS. Not a bad thing in concept. Despite their short shelf life, they do momentarily return us to better living habits, bring our attention to neglected goals: committing to a dreamed-of trip, more visits to the gym, eating more veggies, volunteering at Family Kitchen. Like most such lists, they are often more self-revelatory than we realize. All about me? Others? 50/50? Enter the credo.

Credo? What's that? It's not the same thing as a New Year's resolution, which is more a human-doing goal than a human-being goal. Instead, for my money, a credo is a human-being goal inside which all the human-doing goals can fit. More mantra than memorandum. Your brass ring, true north, all your New Year's resolutions under one roof. Credo comes from the Latin word meaning "I believe" and is the first word of many religious creeds. So, is it a statement of what is? Of what's hoped for? A motto? A manifesto? A note to self or a note to the world? A battle cry? An olive branch? The answer to all these questions is yes and that's no koan or joke. The credo has long since found its way into the boardrooms of businesses, universities, barracks and banks and now applies to any guiding principle or set of principles: Semper Fi, Veritas, The Winds of Freedom Blow, By Work All Things Increase and Grow or, what some jokingly suggest should be Visit Bend's slogan in its commitment to attracting people to town: Veni, Vidi, Velcro.

The idea of a credo as the uber resolution was bandied about at a prenew year gathering of friends, all of a certain age. (We wondered out loud what Gen Xers, Millenials and Digital Natives would say.) The conversation quickly spotlighted the waste-no-timers: "Choose joy," one said immediately—as well as the over-thinkers, stymied by whether a credo is a statement of something absolute and unchanging versus a current situation that needs attention such as "clean air and water for everyone."

The great, inspirational leaders were, no doubt, waste-no-timers. I'd guess their credo was at the tip of their tongue from the get-go. They had a special mission on their earth walk and they knew it. We just recognized the great Martin Luther King on January 16, and were reminded of his powerful, do-or-die mantra, "I have a dream." President John Fitzgerald Kennedy's "Ask not what your country can do for you but what you can do for your country," propelled me into the Peace Corps. Who hasn't been inspired by Eric Hoffer's oft-quoted, "We are made kind by being kind."

What was evident in the responses at the gathering that night is that in phrasing a credo you are stating something about how you move in the world, who you are, what you stand for, where you're headed. Here's an assortment from that evening:

No excuses

Keep the main thing the main thing

Be generous

Embrace chaos

Show up

Be curious

Less is more

Choose happiness

Create space

On January 1, 1943, Woody Guthrie, an American singer-songwriter and one of the most significant figures in American folk music, wrote a list of thirty-three "New Years Rulin's" in his journal. A pop quiz: in reading these, which are resolutions and which are credos? Which, by implication, could include all the rest?

1. *Work more and better*
2. *Work by a schedule*
3. *Wash teeth if any*
4. *Shave*
5. *Take bath*
6. *Eat good — fruit — vegetables — milk*
7. *Drink very scant if any*
8. *Write a song a day*
9. *Wear clean clothes — look good*
10. *Shine shoes*
11. *Change socks*
12. *Change bed cloths often*
13. *Read lots good books*
14. *Listen to radio a lot*
15. *Learn people better*
16. *Keep rancho clean*
17. *Don't get lonesome*
18. *Stay glad*
19. *Keep hoping machine running*
20. *Dream good*
21. *Bank all extra money*
22. *Save dough*
23. *Have company but don't waste time*
24. *Send Mary and kids money*
25. *Play and sing good*
26. *Dance better*
27. *Help win war—beat fascism*
28. *Love mama*

29. *Love papa*
30. *Love Pete*
31. *Love everybody*
32. *Make up your mind*
33. *Wake up and fight*

I'm putting my money on 31, 32 and 33. And you?

CHAPTER 35

Doomsday Dress Rehearsal

IT'S HARD TO PINPOINT EXACTLY when the over-the-hill gang starts reading that particular section of the newspaper, but it seems to start roughly at age sixty. "Not yet," or "Maybe soon," is the closest to a no from sixty-somethings. Otherwise, it's a definite yes in response to my asking "Do you read the obituaries?"

It makes sense, as we oldsters progress through the go-go, slo-go and no-go stages of life, that we likewise migrate from wedding and anniversary announcements to the obits. At first blush it might seem dreary, given the subject matter. Unlike wedding or anniversary notices, an obit is not the heralding of a beginning nor a milestone of something that is ongoing in real time, rather the acknowledgment of *"le point final,"* the end of life's sentence, a death.

But what is alive in the written and online tributes to those who have passed is each individual's purchase and imprint on the world. You can feel the energy of the unique lives described. Such daring, joy, sacrifice, suffering, triumph, purpose! Even if we don't know the deceased, we can identify with their honest effort to stitch together a well-lived and well-loved life in the time they had. We can see our own struggles and ambitions within these brief biographies, can spot a goal of our own that they realized in their lifetime, and we had damn well better get a move-on if we're going to accomplish it in ours.

Today, with obituaries online, notifications can be broadcast instantly and widely. It wasn't always so. The word obituary comes from the Latin "obitus" meaning "going down," "death." The first known public notification of deaths was printed on papyrus in the *Acta Diurna* in 59 BCE in ancient Rome! Flash forward to the 1800s in the U.S. when obituaries became common during the Civil War as a way of notifying relatives of the loss of a loved one. In the 1930s, thanks to better printing presses, obits began to come into their own. Newspaper editors composed elaborate tributes to the most noteworthy citizens (sometimes jumping the gun, as was the case with Mark Twain and Ernest Hemingway—pronounced dead before their time). Commoners, however, were acknowledged but only in passing (no pun intended) with terse death notices that included a death announcement, short biography, list of survivors, and funeral details. That changed when newspapers recognized there was money in them thar deaths and began selling space for obituaries written and submitted by family members. As a result, the commoners' template gave way to a more freeform style, the spotlight and ink shared by the famous with the everyday person. One relatively recent confirmation of this sea change was when, after the September 11, 2001, attacks, the *New York Times* published short narratives on every single one of the three thousand killed. "Everybody was recognized as a whole person," stated obituary expert Susan Soper. You'd think that would go without saying.

At a recent gathering with friends, I quizzed those present apropos of my anecdotal research about obituaries. The ninety-year-old matriarch of the family abruptly got up from the table and disappeared into her study, returning with a very small piece of paper inscribed with the following verse which, she claimed, was included in the 1943 obituary for Elinor Glyn, the captivating author of racy (for the 1930s) romance novels.

Would you like to sin
With Elinor Glyn
On a tiger skin?
Or would you prefer
To err with her
On some other fur?

In contrast to this humorous send-off, but no less engaging, was a recent tribute in the *Bend Bulletin* honoring the life of a woman who dedicated her life to training horses. In 1981 she was the first female to win the Snaffle Bit Futurity. Her favorite horses, Cobra Chex and Lena, are mentioned by name. "Horses not only touch us with their spirit," she was quoted as saying, "but they allow...a brief moment, experiencing freedom on earth—when horse and rider become one."

I am always struck by the exquisite configurations of our snowflake selves. When we put our ear to the seashell of others' lives and listen, really listen, I wonder how in the world we fail to see that we all drink from a common well of humanity? How can these glimpses not inspire us to work toward a common wealth and welcome?

Here's a challenge for millennials and up. Pen your own obituary every year. Write it in the third person. List accomplishments achieved, sure, but more importantly, address how you have manifested in the world to date, leaned into living. It's a mapping exercise to evaluate who, not where, one is relative to the person one would like to be at the conclusion of the final act. This dress rehearsal never fails to chasten and motivate. Ask me how I know.

CHAPTER 36

Indoor Sports

REMEMBER TUESDAYS WITH MORRIE? Published in 1997, it recounted conversations between Morris (Morrie) Schwartz, nearly eighty and
approaching the end stage of ALS, and Mitch Albom, a former student
of Professor Schwartz's at Brandeis. The book sold an astounding fifteen million copies! Why? Rachel Syme, the author of *Pearl Hunting*, in a
January, 2022, issue of the *New Yorker*, ascribes the book's popularity to a
predatory tendency alive and well today: young adults seeking to mine
wisdom from the old. The closer to death's door the older person is, the
more prescient their most clichéd statements are regarded. Syme writes,
"Eager not to waste our lives, we tend to devour lessons from people
approaching the end of theirs. There's something macabre about this
appetite, the way it turns an aging mind into a consumable product." She
calls them "comforting mantras from the edge of existence." "Love each
other or perish," and, "Money is not a substitute for tenderness," are two
of Morrie's.

The hunt for insights from the over-the-hill gang continues today in podcasts, such as *70 Over 70*, and books. One is Stephen Petrow's re-verse-psychology approach in *Stupid Things I Won't Do When I Get Old: A Highly Judgmental, Unapologetically Honest Accounting of All the Things Our Elders Are Doing Wrong*. For young adults it's tricky because they both do and don't want to know what the view is at the brink of death. The sage advice from the graveside, if adhered to, might guarantee a longer life. Then again, there's the possibility that hanging around the elderly might accelerate their own exit.

In case you missed the memo, being old is not something to be avoided nor can you; not a faux pas, staved off with seven thousand steps a day and a Mediterranean diet, hidden with tucks and lifts, and ultimately summed up in platitudes for young adults to live by. Rather, the last part of life can be the best and certainly is the most courageous and inventive. That perspective has been around at least since the 1800s when Robert Browning wrote, "Grow old along with me!/ The best is yet to be./ The last of life, for which the first was made." If Baby Boomers and a grow-ing number of outspoken eighty-year-olds are right, Robert Browning's "best" includes indoor sports, a definite change in tone and topic to the Third Act conversation.

Should the notion of late-in-the-game sex be news to you, there's a spate of information on the subject of keeping pace with graying Boomers in the bedroom. Check out "The Joys (and Challenges) of Sex After 70" in the January 16, 2022, edition of *The New York Times*: "...a quar-ter of participants ages seventy-five to eighty-five said they had sex in the last year...And almost one-quarter...were doing it once a week—or more. Along with pleasure, they may be getting benefits that are linked to sex: a stronger immune system, improved cognitive function, cardiovascu-lar health in women and lower odds of prostate cancer." Or "Sex and Seniors: The 70-Year Itch," *HealthDay*, June 2021: "Use it or lose it," says geriatrics expert Walter M. Bortz. "If you stay interested, stay healthy, stay off medications, and have a good mate, then you can have good sex all the way to the end of life. And although not everyone wants or needs an active sex life, many people continue to be sexual all their lives... ." Or

Jane Fonda's book, *Prime Time*: "If you've loved before, you can love again, and the same is true for sex. If there was a time in your life you enjoyed sex, you can recover that pleasure—if you want to—because Cupid's bow is undeterred by age. In fact it may fly truer and land deeper." A fictional gem on the subject is *Our Souls at Night* by Kent Haruf.

For the children of seniors getting it on, there's a definite "spare me" factor when imagining their older parents, whether long-married or recently re-partnered, engaging in sex. Platitudes on a life well lived, yes. But don't include advice on sex! However, as evidenced in recent books and articles, the ageing population has important words of wisdom to offer on what true intimacy is, what it can be. For all sorts of reasons associated with ageing, conventional ideas of sex no longer apply but when creatively substituted, the experience is the real intimate deal. When someone lovingly traces your lines, you are redrawn. When someone truly loves you for who you are, wrinkles and all, you are truly beheld. And although the exterior packaging might be less than what it was, another pearl confirmed by elders is that they're as adolescent as ever on the inside...hopeful, brash, impetuous, romantic, lonely, and seeking bromides to live by as much as anyone else. The (soap) opera's never over. And that's good news.

CHAPTER 37

Hello Walls

FOR ALL THE COMMERCIAL HYPE OF MERRY and happy, and as all sizes and shapes of "family" try to wriggle into the cultural one-size that's supposed to fit all, for many members of the over-the-hill gang, Yuletide can turn out to be more mono than ménage. For a variety of reasons (treacherous travel, illness, family dynamics, loss of a spouse), it can be a lonely time of year for older people living on their own when family doesn't show up and the usual hubbub is replaced by one hand clapping. In fact, growing older, if you buy into the hype, is guaranteed to be an increasingly solitary and lonely experience. But it doesn't need to be.

First of all, don't believe all the articles on the life-shortening effects of too much alone time when you're older. Sure, there are seismic shifts that take place later in life, often resulting in a more solitary way of life, but loneliness is not an unavoidable by-product. Plus, it turns out oldsters aren't the kings and queens of forsaken, so we can let go of that coveted notion. At what age (twenty? forty? sixty? seventy?) would you say Americans are most lonely? What's your guess? I was surprised by what I found. According to a 2020 study out of the University of California, San Diego, Americans are most lonely in their twenties and least in their sixties.

Sure, it's true. When we're older, living alone can lead to social isolation and that can lead to loneliness, but others can feel lonely without being socially isolated, such as the twenty-year-olds in the study; still others can be socially isolated and happy as clams. So, what's the connection? And what to do about lonely besides getting a puppy?

In his recent *New York Times* column, "I Live Alone. Really, I'm Not That Pathetic," Frank Bruni makes a case for his choice to live "uncoupled, in a house for one." He's not one bit lonely. One in every four households in the U.S. is occupied by someone living alone. Some resist it, some celebrate it. I think the operative here is choice. How you feel about being alone is largely dependent on whether you happened to it, not it to you; you don't feel bushwhacked by unanticipated events, recently or over a lifetime; you actively choose to be the architect of your days, feel a sense of control. Then flying solo becomes a pleasure, a freedom.

In point of fact, we can't really control anything. We know this. But it sure feels better when we think we can. Those living alone who make a Holiday Plan B are prepared, if need be, to hang only one stocking by the fire with care in case, for the reasons listed above, no one shows up. Looking at the road reports, I will write one for myself just in case, to get out ahead of the ambush. Skiing that day would be a fine option. Those who, as they age, proactively anticipate moving into assisted living or to a different community to be closer to their children (and are strategic about what the decision implies) will feel more in charge, less isolated by the decision, less lonely than those who feel they had no purchase on the process.

But what if you didn't anticipate an only Holiday and, post-ambush, find yourself on your own and it was never your plan, and doesn't anyone care, and worms start to seem a fine substitute for the traditional rib roast or Hannukah brisket? What if, in a larger sense, as the result of unanticipated life events, you feel emotionally stranded on a desert island? How, after the fact, can you get out ahead of it?

To ward off lonely, how about taking the perspective that living with alone, long- or short-term, is like any other relationship. It has its ups and downs, requires discipline, planning, love, commitment, imagination, forgiveness, compassion, and flexibility. Couples often struggle to find time for themselves in the space of a day, a few precious moments of quiet. Those living on their own have the opposite challenge—building into their day what couples often have too much of: socialization, people (although I have friends who guard their hard-won solitude like it's gold.)

Earlier in this piece I wrote that we can't control anything. I was wrong. We can control our thoughts, our self-talk. Alone is what you think of it, freeing or lonesome. Here's to the metaphorical one stocking by the fire if it's your choice. If it's not, here's to the robust manifestation of Plan B. May this Holiday Season be the one you choose and, in the meantime, send some cheer in the direction of a twenty-something. They just might be feeling lonely.

CHAPTER 38

Playing the Fool

AN ARTICLE IN THE JANUARY 18, 2021, ISSUE of *The New Yorker* addresses one woman's serious pursuit of painting starting in her sixties. Stepping down from an accomplished career as a professor of history at Princeton, and as the author of seven books and the recipient of countless honors, Nell Painter decided to pursue a BFA from Rutgers followed by an MFA from The Rhode Island School of Design, pursuing both with the same rigor she had approached all else in her life. In her memoir, *Old in Art School: A Memoir of Starting Over,* she describes the shock of discovering that suddenly her race (she is Black) took a back seat to the fact that she was old as the provocation of prejudice. Because of her age she wasn't taken seriously by her instructors, was of no interest to younger fellow students. "It wasn't that I stopped being my individual self or stopped being Black or stopped being female, but that *old*, now linked to my sex, obscured everything else beyond *old lady*."

Let's look at this differently. With all the hostile name-calling and taunts associated with current important debates and protests about racial equality, immigration, politics and the environment, guess what "name" neutralizes, zaps them all, and therefore, might just pave the way for productive conversation? *Old.*

Back to Nell Painter. How many of us shy away from trying something new after age sixty and why is that? We have drunk the cultural Kool-Aid, that's why. Ageism messaging at work. Athletes are considered over-the-hill by age thirty. Middle-aged executives don't dare make a longed-for career change out of fear of age discrimination. Nell Painter experienced firsthand the cultural bias that starting something new later in life is regarded as foolish.

But playing the fool is a good thing, never mind that the Latin origin of the word, follis, cites bellows and windbag—a bit off-putting. But wind is also associated with inspire, to breathe out, to convey a truth or idea. Expanding on that interpretation, the notion of the wise fool first emerged in the 1300s followed by William Shakespeare taking up the fool's cause in the 1500s, elevating the role of the court jester from entertainer to truthteller and scripting many wise fools into his plays. In his *Guide to Shakespeare*, Isaac Asimov sums it up. "The great secret of the successful fool that he is no fool at all."

In tarot card games starting in the fifteenth century (before they were preempted for fortune telling) the fool was the most valuable card. When tarot decks were subsequently used for divination, the fool came to represent new beginnings, faith in the future, and beginner's luck. Given that every day is a new beginning, it figures we all have the same shot at luck each morning, right? In this sense, playing the fool would mean trying new things, staying curious despite the years already invested in the pit- and pratfalls of life, no matter the age. Enter the wise, old fool.

Margaret Talbot, the author of *The New Yorker* article on Painter, suggests that parents (or grandparents, for that matter) who wait patiently for hours in a studio or front hall for their child or grandchild to finish ballet or kick boxing lessons are sending the message they have nothing better to do, that learning new things is reserved for the young. But it doesn't have to be so. Talbot references current studies of what has been dubbed "crystallized intelligence" that show that cognitive skills don't all peak at once, some even improving as we age. "Societal pressure on young adults to specialize and succeed…is as wrongheaded and oppressive on the one end of life as patronizing attitudes toward the old are on the other," says Talbot. She encourages us to remember learning to do something new (skill not fact) "when you didn't really care what your performance of it said about your place in the world, when you didn't know what you didn't know." In short, be foolish.

I rail against this culture's tendency to bundle all that we elders have been, are, hope to be, into one convenient, expedient, dismissive category: old. Like some sort of wireless societal bundling offer for ancients. But if you have managed to follow my (non) logic, the most powerful card in the deck, it turns out, is the elder fool because the moniker "old" upstages and trumps all other limiting and insulting labels. So, let's play the card we've been dealt. Here's to the sage fool! The hardy and hearty old fool! The bold but wise buffoon! By playing the elder card, I wager we can eclipse the destructive name-calling plaguing society today and shift the conversation to a solution-oriented one. Just imagine that! The deck is stacked in favor of us wise old fools.

CHAPTER 39

Chat Me Up

WE OLDER FOLKS ARE KNOWN for relying on our children or their children's children to work out computer and cell phone issues, to teach us how to use the remote, to program this and download that, to interface smart watches with smart phones (thank you, Dick Tracy). With some notable exceptions, and I am decidedly not one, geezers are noted for being behind the times when it comes to technology. Maybe even resistant—longing for, heck yeah, party lines. Remember those? Or dialing the operator. We dialed "O" to make long distance calls until the 1950s. That "O," that voice on the end of the line, was, in a way, the equivalent of our modern-day Google, Alexa, and Siri. Watch out what you ask for.

Since those days it has been a rapidly accelerating technological march toward the now, starting with...When does one start? How about with television, then computers, fax machines (the big joke was to send your children off to college with the instruction to "practice safe fax"...how quaint!), smart phones, laptops, Facebook, Google, Instagram, TikTok, smart cars, Roomba, Eufy. Note how our social habits (posture, average weight) and all the ways we love our neighbors as ourselves have changed along with these so-called advances. And how about the colonization of our vocabulary: social media's LOL, BTW, FYI, DYK, photobombing, swiping, trolling, blogs, vlogs, memes, clickbait, AMA, bot? Streaming has nothing to do with rivers, brooks, creeks or streams.

Now there's another technological kid on the block. A sneaky and in-sidious one, if you ask me..It's touted as the cleverest of its kind thus far. According to an anecdotal survey I conducted over the past week, it's new to most in Bend. I spoke to an eighty-year-old, a middle-aged bank-er, a thirty-something cashier in a natural food store, a twenty-year-old at a mail service shop, a shopper in a grocery outlet, friends at an Oscars gathering, a young checker at the local hardware. The cross section was evenly balanced between men and women, mostly Caucasian except for one Hispanic and one Black American. Ages ranged from twenty to eighty. Two had heard of it but hadn't tried it. Three had used it. The rest had not heard of it at all. Of the three who had checked it out, the shop-per in the grocery outlet (who turned out to be a computer professional) said it was potentially dangerous; the eighty-year-old was intrigued; the banker was hooked on the "digital secretary" it is professed to be. Indeed, according to projections, "it will be possible to build each customer their own customized AI that predicts what they need, responds to them per-sonally, and remembers all their interactions. This isn't science fiction. It is entirely doable with the technology just released," according to Ethan Mollick in the *Harvard Business Review*.

So, what is "it"? It's ChatGPT, an artificial intelligence chatbot devel-oped over the past four years or so by OpenAI. Elon Musk is a co-founder. Microsoft invested $11 billion as of January 2023. It was launched in December 2022 and is soon to be followed by Google's version called Gemini. By January, ChatGPT had amassed one hundred million monthly users in two months. By comparison, it took TikTok nine months to reach one hundred million and Instagram two and one-half years. ChatGPT gets mixed reviews depending on if you read comments from people who, in my opinion, regard the mind solely as a calculating machine

(Kevin Roose of *The New York Times* labeled it, "the best artificial intelligence chatbot ever released to the general public." Samantha Lock of *The Guardian* noted it was able to generate "impressively detailed" and "human-like" text)...versus those who regard human thought and creativity as what defines our humanity. In his blog *The Red Hand Files*, songwriter Nick Cave calls this new form of artificial intelligence "a grotesque mockery of what it is to be human." Others called it "convincing-sounding nonsense, devoid of truth." Last I heard, that was known as bullshit.

Maybe it's because my father wouldn't allow television in our house on the basis we'd eschew reading and forget how to think for ourselves. To me, this bot is more evidence, and a powerful one, that my father was right. It is a tipping point that bodes another fraught change in the social and cultural landscape. Are we at risk of abdicating forming our own thoughts and ideas, of settling for AI artifice? There is no beating heart behind these sentences and paragraphs. In fact, there's no sign of living, breathing intelligence at all. Ask me how I really feel.

CHAPTER 40

Black Ice

SOMETIMES SOMETHING HAPPENS out of the blue that restores your belief everything is right with the world. Moments like these are precious. I recently had one: a friend emailed, instructing me to drop everything, grab my skates, there's black ice at Todd Lake!

I come by my love of black ice honestly. During the winters in New England where I grew up, there was lots of sledding and, of course, skiing, thanks to Rube Goldberg-esque rope tows on every small hill. But best of all, there were always early winter cold snaps that froze ponds and lakes solid, creating what's called black (some call it blue) ice, the result of a magical confluence of unique conditions: "No wind. No snow. No moving water. A slow freeze," as Carrie Tait writes in Toronto's *Globe and Mail*. Here's her scientific explanation of the black ice phenomenon just to up the awe ante. "All ice crystals have six sides, grow from the top down, and bond to their neighbors to form a sheet," explains Tait. "Black ice forms when the crystals grow perpendicular to the surface and parallel to each other...These crystals will be the same size and shape, like a new set of dinner candles perfectly packaged and standing on end. When ice crystals grow vertically and bond perfectly, light passes through without distorting." That glistening chandelier is what's holding you up when you skate on black ice!

It's not just the perfection of moving across such an immaculate surface, not just the ability to see to the bottom of a pond or get lost in the inscrutable dark-eyed beauty of a deeper lake, it's also the songs the ice sings. Sweden's Henrik Trygg has recorded the haunting range of sounds triggered by the weight of skaters gliding across the surface of virgin black ice, a high C reverberation on thinner ice, lower for thicker, like tracing the edge of a full and empty crystal glass with your finger. Then there are the more typical loud moans and thunderclaps caused by the expansion and contraction of ice as temperatures change.

If by now you're ready to join the ranks of the black ice-crazed wild (meaning "naturally occurring") ice brigade, take some precautions. Don't go alone. If you're sixty-five or older, wear a helmet. Head injuries at this late date are not advised (or at any date, for that matter.) Make sure the ice is three inches to four inches thick. Black ice is the strongest. White opaque ice, compromised by snow fall and melting and freezing cycles, is weaker. "Thick and blue, tried and true, white and crispy, way too risky," as the old saw goes.

As a kid, I'd watch my mother glide across a sable Lake Cochichewick in Massachusetts wearing her ancient toe curl skates. She would gracefully execute school figures on a single edge...a figure eight or a three turn with one leg extended gracefully. I'd skitter behind with double runners strapped to my snow boots or, more likely, lie on my stomach and stare down at the mysterious aquatic world beneath me. Fast forward decades to winters ranching along the Yellowstone River in Montana, miles of dark glass solid under my skates; next, in Oregon, far-flung neighbors gathering for crack-the-whip on Prineville Reservoir; then, that unforgettable winter when Summer Lake froze with smooth, black ice sections snaking between ghoulish ice confections pushed up and freeze-framed by the wind; and of course, those times Todd Lake turned into a frozen mirror, reflecting the cradling steep slopes and trees. *In Too Cold to Snow*, a delightful and spirited memoir of growing up in Bend in the 1950s, author Sue Fountain chronicles the frigid winter days that reliably preceded the heavy snows. Troy Field would be flooded, according to Fountain, and young and old would gather to skate.

Who could have imagined then Todd Lake's black ice, or any wild ice anywhere, would now be such a rarity. But it is, as the recent United Nations Climate Change Conference underscored with plentiful evidence—we're skating on thinner and thinner ice.

After getting word of Todd Lake's black ice, I excitedly readied for an early morning departure, packing the car with skates, helmet, and an old wooden kitchen chair to use while getting skates on and off, and to push in front of me on the ice as I gained stability, a tried-and-true, if indecorous, workaround. But that night it snowed, then a sudden rise in temperatures, then rain. Todd Lake's black ice was gone in an instant. Sometimes something happens out of the blue to remind you of your stake in helping right the world.

CHAPTER 41

Mind Your Commas

I HAVE A FEELING NONE OF YOU currently have (or ever had) *Eats, Shoots & Leaves* on the top of your must-read list, especially considering the subtitle: "The Zero Tolerance Approach to Punctuation." It sounds boring but trust me, Lynne Truss's book, first published in the early 2000s and still going strong, is hysterically funny.

The author is no flash in the pan. She has many novels and children's books to her credit, is a book reviewer for London's *The Sunday Times* and a regular on the BBC. As a dramatist, Truss is also known for her riotous wit as the author of numerous radio comedies. But a book based on a misplaced comma an international bestseller? Come on!

It's true. *Eats, Shoots & Leaves* is hilarious history and, considering careless usage and low standards in e-mail, text messages and on the Internet, is a droll reminder of what an important thing the correct placement of punctuation is. The inspiration for this frolic resulted from Truss coming across a misplaced comma that called into question the presumed gentle nature of the giant panda bear. Here's how Truss sets up the scene:

"A panda walks into a cafe. He orders a sandwich, eats it, then draws a gun and fires two shots in the air.

"Why?" asks the confused waiter, as the panda makes towards the exit. The panda produces a badly punctuated wildlife annual and tosses it over his shoulder.

"I'm a panda," he says, at the door. "Look it up."

The waiter turns to the relevant entry and, sure enough, finds an explanation.

Panda. Large black-and-white bear-like mammal, native to China. Eats, shoots and leaves."

The only thing the poor panda ever really wanted to do was to eat bamboo shoots and leaves, but an errant comma in an annual report turned him into a gunslinger. Who knew the comma was such a gamechanger. No doubt! No, doubt! Don't stop now! Don't, stop now! Or this, offered by Truss, "Leonora walked on her head, a little higher than usual." The right answer? Leonora walked on, her head a little higher than usual. And then there's net zero versus net, zero.

I'm acquainted with a retired couple who live in a small town in rural Central Oregon. Their favorite getaway is not the big city, rather a cabin in an even more remote high desert location. Despite logistics and distances, these two are committed to living net zero (defined by the United Nations as cutting greenhouse gas emissions as close to zero as possible). If it's good enough for the U.N., it's good enough for this dedicated duo. They recognize the positive accumulative effect of individual actions for the good of the planet, that each reduced carbon footprint is a step forward. Their residence operates on solar energy with any excess exported to the electric grid. There, it either earns them a credit or reduces the load on local electricity, saving money for all residents in the area. In addition, they have installed a small, grid-tied solar array at their cabin and charging stations at both their home and their cabin to accommodate their electric pickup.

If you're tired of singing *Cry Me an Atmospheric River*, there are lots of ways to get to the golden goose egg besides going solar or ditching your gas mobile(s). Eat more fruits, nuts and plants (or bamboo, if you're channeling your inner panda); use public transportation when available; if not already in place, encourage your community to offer compost collection services to reduce food waste; plant more trees while preserving existing trees. (FYI, the goals of Bend's Vision Action Plan 2024-2028 feature "Solarizing Bend" and "Thriving Urban Tree Canopy" defined as "... no net tree loss and an equitable canopy cover citywide.") And, of course, reduce trash any way you can. Colorado's Center for Science Education has determined, "landfills are, in fact, the third largest source of methane emissions in the U.S., behind natural gas/petroleum use and animals raised for food production (and their manure). In the U.S., each member of a household produces an average of 4.4 pounds of trash per day. That's 1,660 pounds of trash per person per year!"

Before you contact me to let me know I urgently need to get out more often because I am worried about misplaced commas, let us old methane producers (get it?) instead commit to doing whatever we can to achieve net zero before reaching the "point final," the end of life's sentence, the inevitable net, zero...not to put too fine a comma on it.

CHAPTER 42

Kinder, Gentler

THERE'S OFTEN A HARD EDGE to New Year's resolutions. A punitive subtext. A get with it, do more, do better tone. If ever there was a year for a kinder, gentler take on being our best selves, 2024 might just be it.

I am not a birder, not by a stretch, though I am devoted to the winged victories that inhabit my feeders. I try my best to distinguish between, as birdwatchers refer to them, the LBBs (Little Brown Bird) or LBJs (Little Brown Jobs), the look-alike small brown passerines. I can identify some of the most common species: Steller's and scrub Jays, mourning and ring-necked doves, Cassin's finch with its happenin' red crew cut. And during warmer weather, the evening grosbeak is hard to miss with its impressive schnoz and fierce yellow eyebrow.

A couple of weeks ago the big news from a birder friend was that a flock of pine grosbeaks had been spotted on Vicksburg Avenue. I manage a tentative, "Wow?" I'd never heard of a pine grosbeak. I look them up in my bird book. Turns out the pine is a fancy finch, while the evening grosbeak is cousin to the cardinal. Real birders know this stuff and more.

To wit, a 2022 *TIME* magazine article references birder Joan Straussmann who can "rattle off trivia about birds as quickly as a peregrine falcon can blast through the sky." Who knew that "...northern flickers coax their young to leave their nests by continuously shrieking? That American coots sometimes sneak eggs into other hens' nests? That white brows on a male white-throated sparrow indicate he might be a philanderer?"

I read about the pine grosbeak's summer preference for pine forests. Maybe I'd seen them in the Cascades while hiking? Maybe in winter at feeders serving up sunflower seeds? They are certifiably plump, their beak is stubbier than the evening grosbeak's, their head rounder. The male wears a reddish cloak over his head and chest, like chain mail made of tiny feathers. The female's version—a pale yellow shawl. Both have contrasting gray wings with white bars. They aren't supposed to be all that hard to spot. Maybe, I think, I'll go look for them tomorrow.

"Tomorrow" is one of those carefully choreographed days: gym, deadlines, errands. Do more, do better. Adding a bird quest into the mix would be the antithesis of efficiency, and the more relaxed time of day is after bird bedtime. I make my way to Vicksburg anyway, between bank and before groceries. A mini mutiny. My attention turns to the sky: ducks, geese, a flock of smaller birds doing acrobatics far overhead. Could they be...? I pull over and stop, adjust my binoculars. No idea.

My heart rate and MPH both slow as I poke around side streets, study the treetops. Top-down is a refreshing perspective on the town I'd lived in for so long. Given the inexplicable fun this is, I feel compelled to recruit everyone I see. Here comes a couple, she with walking sticks, he pulled along by an overeager dog. I roll down my window. "I hear there's a flock of pine grosbeaks in your neighborhood. Have you seen them?" Though they confess they wouldn't know one if they did, they prattle enthusiastically about the popularity of their bird feeder as winter sets in. Next, a woman with two large German shepherds who both give me a no-false-moves look. No, she hasn't seen the grosbeaks, but, "How exciting! I'll keep an eye out!"

When do I stop and randomly talk to strangers? Who knew an impromptu birding expedition would produce a heightened sense of community? Look how a small, feathered common cause is a bridge to friendly conversation. I continue on my lollygagging way, beguiled by the gentleness of being off-purpose, the lockstep of my schedule giving way to something ineffable. Who says the shortest distance between two points is a straight line?

Unbeknownst to me, I was verifying a host of studies on the beneficial effects of birdwatching or, in my case, bird looking-for. One, published in *Scientific Reports*, found that seeing or hearing birds improved mental wellbeing for up to eight hours. The National Institutes of Health maintains birdwatching increases oxytocin secretion, results in more efficient brain activity. If that's true, I should accomplish my remaining errands more efficiently than ever and love doing them. Sometimes you go faster when you take your foot off the gas.

CHAPTER 43

Standard Bearers

AS IT TURNED OUT, ON THE NIGHT of the 2024 presidential election, I wound up driving south and east on highway 205, on my way to meet with a couple whose ranch lies on the Oregon/Nevada border. Over the course of the past two years, I have been interviewing people throughout the southeastern corner of the high desert on behalf of the Oregon Desert Land Trust (ODLT), a nonprofit predicated on the conservation of wild and working lands for people and wildlife.

The aim of the bimonthly *Sharing Common Ground* series is to illustrate all the ways it's possible to love the same thing differently. As ODLT's website explains, these interviews profile "those who know and care deeply about this special place. Some make their living in the high desert, some seek out its rivers and canyons to recreate, still others seek solace in the wide open spaces. Though perspectives differ, what all have in common is a love of this landscape. ODLT's goal is to have people's stories, insights, and values resonate with others to increase the appreciation and stewardship of desert communities."

The operative word here is "love" as in win/win, what's best for most;

not my-way-or-the-highway. What ODLT has accomplished in just seven years is truly impressive. Don't believe me? Just ask critters, birds, fish and folks on both sides of the fence.

As I drove through the dark on the empty two-lane road, I frantically scrolled between radio stations, my efforts only producing static. Try as I did, I couldn't get any radio updates on how the history-making night was going. Cell service? Forget about it.

After overnighting in Fields, I continued on to my meeting with the young, fifth generation ranching couple. Their operation takes in carefully managed lower elevation basin grasslands as well as upper country range and healthy wildlife habitat in the Trout Creek Mountains—including high, cold streams that sustain the endangered Lahontan Cutthroat Trout.

A poet at heart, I was moved to write a poem about that night's drive and the meeting that followed.

Static

Presidential Election 2024

Ellen Waterston

*Remote highway in southeastern Oregon, late on a moonless November
night. Here and there, my headlights might illuminate a reflective sign:
    wildlife refuge, wilderness area.*

*That's about it. I tune in for news of my country's fate but only get static.
Who's winning, I wonder? The road ahead looks empty and dark.
    But just then, out of the pitch,*

*a mysterious single, bobbing beam coming at me, too high, too slow
for anything I can name. I tell myself I'm thankful for any emissary of light.
    Closing in,*

*it turns out my redeemer's a solo cowboy at a trot, headlamp secured
above his brim, rifle and lasso strapped to the saddle horn. Maybe looking
    for strays? Putting venison*

in the freezer? Returning home after a visit with a far-flung neighbor?
Does he wonder who's winning? I tune in for news of our shared
country's fate but only get static.

Driving the next day, I reflect on the dwindling Lahontan cutthroat trout; take
pleasure in the golden rabbitbrush, the snow-dusted Pueblos,

the skulking coyote, the Angus grazing in the meadows. I tune in for news
of their habitat's fate but only get static.

At last I'm there. The sign on the gate says their pit bulls don't take kindly
to liberals. I knock anyway and go in, only to find lap dogs and common cause
with the land

we love in common. There's no discussion of winners, of losers, only doers
in the race to conserve the grand scheme of all things wild and working.

We turn off the static.

I offer this because, win, lose or draw, it strikes me that the critically important job for all of us who have lived more than six decades is that of standard bearers of respectful and conciliatory discourse. There will be plenty of winning, losing and drawing to go around; enough fool's gold to keep us all prospecting for years; more easily made, easily broken pie crust promises than you can shake a rolling pin at. Boomers are old enough to know common ground is the only high ground if we hope to survive as a democratic, indivisible nation. What the world needs now, is…you know the lyrics.

All catchphrases aside, let's turn off the static and sing.

Acknowledgments

I am profoundly grateful to Aaron Switzer, publisher of *The Source Weekly*, for his unwavering support of this experiment, from columns to collection; Source Media for publishing *We Could Die Doing This*; *The Source Weekly* editor, Nicole Vulcan, for holding me to deadlines and setting the bar high as a.journalist and professional; book designer, Thomas Osborne, for his impeccable creativity and unflagging patience with this project; night sky photographer, Richard Scott Nelson, whose arresting image appears on the cover of *We Could Die Doing This*; noted authors Judith Barrington, Andrea Carlisle, and Caryl and Jay Casbon for their generous reviews; copy editor, Kharli Rose, for her efficiency and precision; line editors, Floy and Richard Sitts, for catching edits the rest of us missed; publicist, Louise Hawker, for her attention to production and publicity details; Ideas to Inks for the creation of promotional materials; and last but never least, to my three children who often make fun of their mother's mantra—"We could die doing this!"—that she first uttered when on one (of many) hair-raising adventures with them.

Suggested Reading

Albom, Mitch. *Tuesdays with Morrie: An Old Man, A Young Man and Life's Greatest Lesson*. New York: Doubleday Publishing, 1977.

Allende, Isabel. *Aphrodite, A Memoir of the Senses*. New York: Harper Collins, 1999.

Asimov, Isaac. *Asimov's Guide to Shakespeare: A Guide to Understanding and Enjoying the Works of Shakespeare*. Sellersville, Pennsylvania: Avenel, 1978.

Baumeister, Roy F. and Ellen Bratslavsky and Catrin Finkenauer and Kathleen D. Vohs. "Bad is Stronger Than Good." *Review of General Psychology*. 2001.

Bowler, Kate. *No Cure for Being Human: (And Other Truths I Needed to Hear)*. New York: Random House, 2021.

Bruni, Frank. "I Live Alone. Really, I'm Not That Pathetic." *The New York Times*, December 9, 2022. https://www.nytimes.com/2022/12/09/opinion/living-alone-single.html

Cave, Nick. *The Red Hand Files*. https://www.theredhandfiles.com

Chatwin, Bruce. *The Songlines*. New York: Penguin Books, 1988.

Colston, Penelope. "The Finnish Secret to Happiness? Knowing When You Have Enough." *The New York Times*, April 1, 2023.

Combs, Amanda. "What Percentage of Baby Boomers and Seniors Are Gay?" *InSeniors*, June.13, 2023.

Downing, Michael. *Spring Forward: The Annual Madness of Daylight Saving Time*. Berkeley, California: Counterpoint Press. 2005.

Emmons, Cai. "Wrapping Up a Life." Caiemmonsauthor.com. December 28, 2022. https://caiemmonsauthor.com/wrapping-up-a-life

Evans, Paul. KVAL, Eugene, Oregon. May 21, 2021.

Fonda, Jane. *Prime Time*. New York: Penguin Random House, 2012.

Ford, Jamie. *Hotel on the Corner of Bitter and Sweet*. New York: Ballantine Books, 2009.

_____*The Many Daughters of Afong Moy*. New York: Atria Books, 2022.

Fountain, Sue. *Too Cold to Snow: A Memoir*. CreateSpace Independent Publishing Platform, 2013.

Glyn, Elinor. "Elinor Glyn Dies; Novelist, aged 78. Self-Styled 'High Priestess of God of Love.' Shocked Many Readers on 2 Continents." *The New York Times*, September 24, 1943. https://timesmachine.nytimes.com/timesmachine/1943/09/24/issue.html

Gupta, Sanjay. *Keep Sharp: Build a Better Brain at Any Age*. New York: Simon & Schuster, 2021.

Guthrie, Woody. "New Years Rulin's." 1943. https://www.woodyguthrie.org/newyearsrulins.htm

Hafiz, Mohammed. "It Felt Love." *The Illuminated Hafiz: Love Poems for the Journey to Light*. Louisville, Colorado: Sounds True, 2019.

Haruf, Kent. *Our Souls at Night*. New York: Vintage Contemporaries, 2016.

Hollis, James. *Finding Meaning in the Second Half of Life: How to Finally, Really Grow Up*. New York: Avery, 2006.

_____*Prisms: Reflections on the Journey We Call Life*. Asheville, North Carolina: Chiron Publications, 2021.

Howard, Josh, Producer/Director. *The Lavender Scare: The Untold Story of a Brutal Witch Hunt and the Courageous Few Who Fought Back*. Full Exposure Films, 2019. https://www.thelavenderscare.com)

Hempton, Gordon. *One Square Inch of Silence: One Man's Search for Natural Silence in a Noisy World*. New York: Free Press, 2009.

Johnson, David. *The Lavender Scare: The Cold War Persecution of Gays and Lesbians in the Federal Government*. Chicago: University of Chicago Press, 2006.

Jones, Maggie. "The Joys (and Challenges) of Sex After 70." *The New York Times*, January 12, 2022. https://www.nytimes.com/2022/01/12/magazine/sex-old-age.html

Keith, Toby. *Don't Let the Old Man In*. Show Dog-Universal Music, 2018.

Kondo, Marie. *The Life-Changing Magic of Tidying Up: The Japanese Art of Decluttering and Organizing*. Berkeley, California: Ten Speed Press, 2014.

Lexa, Rebecca. "Existence Value: Why All of Nature is Important Whether We Can Use It or Not," October 16, 2023. https://rebeccalexa.com/existence-value

Lift Every Voice Oregon https://www.lifteveryvoiceoregon.com

Magnusson, Margareta. *The Gentle Art of Swedish Death Cleaning: How to Free Yourself and Your Family from a Lifetime of Clutter*. New York: Scribner, 2018.

Martin, Tracie. "Forever, Wherever, Whenever: How Technology Has Changed Obituaries.".National Newspaper Foundation Association. February 1, 2024. https://www.nna.org/forever-wherever-whenever-how-technology-has-changed-obituaries

Maynes-Aminzade, Liz. "Will Shortz's Life in Crossword." *The New Yorker*, February 15, 2023. https://www.newyorker.com/culture/the-new-yorker-interview/will-shortzs-life-in-crosswords

Mollick, Ethan. "ChatGPT Is a Tipping Point for AI." *Harvard Business Review*, December 14, 2022.

Naughton, Charlotte. "A trip to Switzerland in search of a good death." *The Guardian*, November 20, 2021. https://www.theguardian.com/society/2021/nov/20/a-trip-to-switzerland-in-search-of-a-good-death-all-this-instead-of-just-doing-it-in-brighton

Newcomb, Beth. "Short cycles of a low-calorie diet that replicates fasting appeared to reduce inflammation and delay cognitive decline in mouse models of Alzheimer's disease; initial data indicates diet's safety in Alzheimer's patients." USC Leonard Davis School of Gerontology Study.

September 27, 2022. https://gero.usc.edu/author/beth-newcomb

Nussbaum, Jeff. "Trump's Jokes Killed DC's Sense of Humor." *Politico*, April 22, 2024.

Olmstead, Molly. "The Most Influential 80-Plus-Year-Olds in America," *SLATE*, December 22, 2020. https://slate.com/human-interest/2020/12/80-over-80-most-influential-top-20.html

Painter, Nell. *Old in Art School: A Memoir of Starting Over*. Berkeley, California: Counterpoint, 2018.

Petrow, Stephen. *Stupid Things I Won't Do When I Get Old: A Highly Judgmental, Unapologetically Honest Accounting of All the Things Our Elders Are Doing Wrong*. New York: Citadel, 2021.

Pollan, Michael. *How to Change Your Mind: What the New Science of Psychedelics Teaches Us About Consciousness, Dying, Addiction, Depression, and Transcendence*. New York: Penguin Press, 2018.

Radvansky, Gabriel. "Walking through doorways causes forgetting, new research shows." *Notre Dame News*, November 16, 2011. https://news.nd.edu/news/walking-through-doorways-causes-forgetting-new-research-shows

Rilke, Rainier Maria. *Letters to a Young Poet*. London, United Kingdom: Merchant Books,.2012.

Ravikumar, Vandana. "'I don't want them anymore.'– Ben Beers. Oregon dad has guns destroyed after Texas school shooting." *Tacoma News Tribune*, May 27, 2022.

Richardson, Heather Cox. "Letters from an American." Substack, November 9, 2022.

Roach, Margaret. "After a Frantic Year, It's Time for 'Slow Birding'." *The New York Times*, December 24, 2022.

Robinson, Kim Stanley. *The Ministry for the Future*. New York: Orbit US, 2020.

Rodriguez, Tori. "Laugh Lots, Live Longer." Cognition, September 1, 2016. https://www.scientificamerican.com/article/laugh-lots-live-longer

Roose, Kevin. "A Conversation with Bing's Chatbot Left Me Deeply Unsettled." *The New York Times*, February 16, 2023. https://www.

nytimes.com/2023/02/16/technology/bing-chatbot-microsoft-chatgpt.html

Rossato-Bennett, Michael, Director. *Alive Inside: A Story of Music and Memory.* Full Exposure Films, 2014. http://www.aliveinside.us/#land

Simmons, Philip. *Learning to Fall: The Blessings of an Imperfect Life.* New York: Bantam, 2003.

Stafford, Kim. "Poems for a Cause." As the Sky Begins to Change. California: Red Hen Press, 2024.

Stahl, Lesley. "Health Care Challenges for Trans Gender Youth." *60 Minutes,* May 23, 2021. https://www.cbsnews.com/video/transgender-health-care-60-minutes-video-2021-05-23

Syme, Rachel. "Pearl Hunting." *The New Yorker,* January 3&10, 2022. https://www.newyorker.com/magazine/2022/01/03

Tait, Carrie. "On a frozen mountain lake in B.C., a skating rink that goes on forever." *The Globe and Mail,* December 15, 2017. https://www.theglobeandmail.com/news/british-columbia/skating-on-black-ice-on-a-frozen-bclake/article37353580

Talbot, Margaret. "Is It Really Too Late to Learn New Skills?" *The New Yorker,* January 11, 2021. https://www.newyorker.com/magazine/2021/01/18/is-it-really-too-late-to-learn-new-skills

Tillotson, Kristin. "More Older Women Coming Out as Lesbians." *Cape Cod Times,* January 15, 2010. https://www.capecodtimes.com/site-map/2010/january/15

The Peaceful Presence Project. https://thepeacefulpresenceproject.org

Truss, Lynn. *Eats, Shoots and Leaves: The Zero Tolerance Approach to Punctuation.* New York: Avery. 2003.

Tugend, Alina. "Praise Is Fleeting, but Brickbats We Recall." *The New York Times,* March 23, 2012. https://www.nytimes.com/2012/03/24/your-money/why-people-remember-negative-events-more-than-positive-ones.html

Waterston, Ellen. *Where the Crooked River Rises,* OSU Press, Corvallis, Oregon, 2010. (an excerpt from the chapter titled "That's Deep" is included in Chapter 2 of *We Could Die Doing This*)

Waterston, George C. *Order and Counter Order*. New York: Philosophical Library, 1966.

Willoughby, Gail. "The 70-Year Itch." *Seniors Lifestyle*, June 22, 2018. https://seniorslifestylemag.com/health-well-being/seniors-and-the-70-year-itch

About the Author

Award-winning author and poet Ellen Waterston has published four poetry and four literary nonfiction titles, including most recently, *Hotel Domilocos: Poems* and *Walking the High Desert: Encounters with rural America along the Oregon Desert Trail*. She is founder of the Writing Ranch which, since 2000, has conducted workshops for established and emerging writers, and of the annual Waterston Desert Writing Prize, launched in 2015 and adopted in 2019 as a program of the High Desert Museum. In 2024 she was appointed to a two-year term as the eleventh Oregon Poet Laureate and awarded both the Literary Arts of Portland's Stewart H. Holbrook and Soapstone Bread and Roses awards, recognizing her work as an author and advocate for the literary arts. She is the author of the *Common Ground* series, an Oregon Desert Land Trust interview project conducted in southeastern Oregon. Awards and recognitions include the WILLA in both nonfiction and poetry, Foreword finalist in literary nonfiction, winner of the Obsidian Prize in Poetry, and an honorary Ph.D. in Humane Letters from Oregon State University Cascades, where she serves as guest faculty in the Low Residency MFA in Creative Writing. She lives in Central Oregon.

PHOTO: SAVANNAH MENDOZA